MEGAN MCKENNA

MOUTHY

JB

JOHN BLAKE

Published by John Blake Publishing,
an imprint of Kings Road Publishing
2.25 The Plaza,
535 Kings Road,
Chelsea Harbour,
London SW10 0SZ

www.johnblakebooks.com
www.facebook.com/johnblakebooks
twitter.com/jblakebooks

First published in Hardback in 2018

ISBN: HB – 978 1 78606 895 8
TPB – 978 1 78606 967 2
Ebook – 978 1 78606 985 6

British Library Cataloguing-in-Publication Data:
A catalogue record for this book is available from the British Library.

Designed and set by seagulls.net

Printed and bound in Great Britain by Clays Ltd, Elcograf S.p.A

1 3 5 7 9 10 8 6 4 2

Papers used by John Blake Publishing are natural, recyclable products made
from wood grown in sustainable forests. The manufacturing processes
conform to the environmental regulations of the country of origin.

Every attempt has been made to contact the relevant copyright-holders, but some
were unobtainable. We would be grateful if the appropriate people could contact us.

John Blake Publishing is an imprint of Bonnier Publishing
www.bonnierpublishing.com

DUDLEY PUBLIC LIBRARIES

The loan of this book may be renewed if not required by other readers, by contacting the library from which it was borrowed.

CP/494

MEGAN MCKENNA

MOUTHS

This book is dedicated to my granddad,
my biggest fan. I love you.

Hi guys,

It's Megan here, and I can't wait to share with you my
stories – there's some really funny ones, a few really
painful ones and yeah, there's probz a few 'WTF' moments
in there too. God, I'm dreading you getting to the 'Mental
Meg' chapters. But come on, girls, I know you all have an
inner psycho too.

You might be thinking, 'Why's she writing her memoir
already? Isn't she about eighteen or something?' Well, I'm
twenty-five actually, and what can I tell you? I've packed
a lot in during those years, and I want to share as much
of it as possible with you while it's all fresh in my mind,
especially now that I'm about to start a brand new chapter
in my life. Of course, you already know what that is –
country singing superstar!

Plus, as you probably already know, I love chatting to all
my followers on social media – well, the nice ones anyway
– and I've noticed you're always asking me questions. I try
to reply to as many as I can, but I don't always feel like I've

answered properly – 280 characters isn't a lot, is it? – so here's my chance to give you a bit more.

I've been unbelievably lucky in my life already – with the family I was born into, the friends I've made, the people I've had the chance to work with, even bumping into people out of the blue, leading to massively amazing opportunities. Louis Walsh... I'll never forget that thing you said just at the right moment. You probably had no idea of the effect it would have on my life. Well, you will now!

Just like there is with everyone, there's been loads of times where I could have gone down the wrong path. When I was thinking about joining *TOWIE*, me going on there was looking pretty unlikely. I didn't even know it at the time, but they'd never had someone with a high profile from another TV show – and I'd already made my name by then on *Celebrity Big Brother*.

And getting to be on *CBB* was completely unexpected as well. My manager Jade (the best manager in the world) didn't tell me when we went for that first meeting, but there was only a really small chance they were going to invite me on the show. They already had an Essex girl on there – the lovely GC – and they already had someone from my series of *Ex on the Beach*, Scotty T, so the chances of me getting on there were tiny. But it happened. And it's all in here.

Plus, when have you ever heard of an Essex girl turning up in Nashville with her Chanel boots, her LV luggage and a blue cape suit to write and record country music, let alone sing the national anthem in the middle of a Tennessee rodeo? But I did, and I have. How I managed all that is in here too.

So yeah, it's been amazing, but I've also had some big challenges along the way. In this book, I'm going to tell you all about my health problems ever since I was child, and the massive impact they've had, and continue to have, on my life. But I hope I can show you how having a serious medical condition doesn't need to get in your way as long as you don't let it.

Also, for the first time, I'm going to tell you all about the bullying I suffered when I was younger. People think I'm mouthy these days – well okay, I am – but that wasn't always the case. It might surprise you to learn how quiet and scared I was when I had to face a bunch of bullies every single day at school, and it's still a time in my life that's really hard and painful to talk about. But I know how important it is to bring stuff like this out in the open. There might be someone reading this who's going through exactly the same thing, and I hope that by seeing how I got through it, well, I really hope it inspires you to see that you can too. Don't let them win!

Another reason for writing this book is to clear up a few things... There's been so much written about me and my life that's not true, and is in fact complete rubbish. So I promise that everything in this book is all true... well, from where I'm sitting anyway, LOL.

This book is also my way of saying thank you to those people who've stuck by me through thick and thin: the ones who know not to believe those headlines (well, not all of them, anyway!); the ones who've made me a cup of tea and given me a shoulder to cry on whenever my heart got broken; the ones who never let me give up on my dream and made me always believe in myself. One thing you'll definitely see in all of the pages of this book is just how much I love my family – they are literally everything to me. And my mates are very special too. So this is a love letter to all of them, and also to Essex, the place that made me and where I'm never going to leave.

Now I know this may come as a shock, but... I'm not perfect, ha ha. In all of these stories there's going to be times when I want to put at the end of every sentence, 'Oh, and by the way, make sure you do as I say, not as I did here.' And there's going to be loads of times when you're going to want to shout at me, 'Nooo, Megan, don't do it, Megan.' Whenever that happens, feel free to throw this book across your bedroom or onto the floor of the Tube – if you're anything like me, you'll be on your sun lounger, so just make sure it doesn't go in the pool! But wherever you happen to be, I beg you to keep on reading, because trust me, I've somehow got there in the end. I'm still here to tell the tale. We all live and learn, right? And if I hadn't made such massive mistakes along the way, well then, there'd be no story and no book, or at least not an interesting one, which I hope it is.

I've gone on long enough here. Time to start the story. I hope this book makes you realise that anything's possible if you want something bad enough and you're prepared to work your arse off for it... Dream big.

Love Megan XX

Prologue

'This is Big Brother. Would Megan come to the diary room immediately?'

Fuuuccccckk!

Somehow, after years and years of effort, hundreds of auditions, long train journeys to and from stage school and a lot of rejection along the way, huge sacrifices by my parents, my nan and granddad, never-ending support from my family, I'd finally made it and got myself into the *Celebrity Big Brother* house so I could finally make a name for myself.

This wasn't just my big break, my chance to show the world how far I'd come. I had millions of people watching my every move. And I was officially losing my shit.

As well as having massive meltdowns, left, right and centre, including rows about tidying clothes away, cleaning up and... mashed potato, what else? I'd finally had enough of housemate John Partridge and his conniving little ways, so I was giving him an earful.

'Fuck off, you little c*nt. He's a little fucking shit. I swear down I'll go sick on that c*nt. You are a nasty piece of shit.'

Plus, talking to one of the other girls...

'Lick the fucking shit out of John's arsehole, mate.'

Wow. Bet you thought, What a little tramp! So now here I was in the diary room, trying to explain myself, but that was all going a bit wrong too...

'It is flipping me out cos he's lied all night and he slates Tiffany, slates Tiffany to the ground, slates her. This fucking bullshit.'

Big Brother's voice boomed out again at me, to the point where I whacked the camera, got restrained by security and removed from the main house.

And just like that, live on national television in front of millions of people, living the so-called dream, years of professional stage training behind me, what was I doing? I'd officially lost it.

So how had everything in my life come to this? Well, let me tell you...

'That's right, Megan, reel him in, reel him in, that's it, easy does it. Perfect. Okay, now throw him back in.'

Say the name Megan McKenna, and I bet the first picture that comes into your head isn't a little girl sitting fishing with her granddad. But that's me, and whenever I look back on my childhood, it's one of the first images I have in my head.

I can still hear my granddad's voice, from those summers that went on and on when I was young. We'd be sat down by the lake, with him teaching me how to fish. Whenever we got a bite, we'd shout our heads off. As you'll be able to tell in this book, I adored my granddad. We'd sit there for hour after hour, just fishing, throwing them back in, and talking. This is probably one of the only sports you'd ever see me doing... Wait, is it even a sport? I don't even know.

Whoops! I'm only on the second page and I've already jumped ahead in the story. Let's start at the very beginning... I was born in Barking, the Barking Hospital to be exact, on 26 September 1992. That makes me a true Essex girl. Not going to lie, I was quite a chubby baby. Okay, to be completely honest, I had rolls of fat – proper ROLLS and loads of them – and I also had a massive head of black, really thick hair. God, I'm really selling myself, aren't I?! My mum used to say I was really cute, and I even remember there was a picture of me in our kitchen, bang in the middle of the kitchen, right above the microwave so nobody could miss it. I used to get so embarrassed – whenever my friends came round, I'd smack it down.

I know I don't need to tell any *TOWIE* fans this next bit, but just for the record, my mum is Tanya, and my dad is Dave. My mum is literally my best friend. I definitely got my party genes from my dad and they both mean the world to me. My mum and dad have been together since they were seventeen years old – they went to the same school, the same class, everything! All those years side by side – pretty impressive, I know. One of these days, I might even get to experience something like that in my own love life. Oh God, let's not go there right now. Moving along...

My mum's always been a florist and my dad used to be a printer. When I was little, we lived in South Woodford in Essex, but all my family on both sides are from Bethnal Green. Proper Cockneys, which is why I probably sound a bit... I don't want to use the word chavvy... Okay, I sound chavvy. I joke about it to Mum – I tell her it's all her fault. She sounds like a proper East Ender, and all my dad's family do too.

We've always been a tight family, and on my dad's side it's huge. He's got three sisters and four brothers, and they all used to live in a two-bedroom flat, all in bunk beds like one of them nursery rhymes or fairy tales. He used to tell me funny stories about when he was little, all of them growing up in that tiny space – I was always saying, 'Tell me about the time... ' But the truth is, they were proper poor. They had literally nothing, and what they did have was shared between eight of them. My mum's family was a bit more stable. They had a flat near Roman Road Market, which is where I spent a lot of time growing up myself, always hanging out at my nan and granddad's house. All of us proper East Enders.

Sadly, my dad lost his parents quite young and moved in with my mum's family when he was eighteen. They were still in Bethnal Green back then, but pretty much straight after, they moved further out of London to South Woodford, and then five years later, to their home in Woodford – where they live to this day. All TOWIE fans would recognise their kitchen table straight away. It's where I've sat for all them scenes, drinking tea and constantly trying to defend myself, ha ha.

I was the first child to come along. My brother Harry arrived three years after me. He was a little shit – he used to eat mud, hide from my mum, and one time he even stuck a runner bean up his nose and we had to rush to A&E so it could get pulled out with tweezers. I'll never forget that image of my little brother getting a full-length green bean pulled out. These days we're really protective of each other – you'd think he was my older brother. To be honest, I'm quite lucky, cos it's like I have my own security guard. To make things even better, he's got an unreal girlfriend who is a really close friend of mine, Jordan.

Then Milly turned up four years after Harry. Poor Milly, I used to drag her around in my Baby Born buggy and walk around with her on my hip like she was my own child. I'll never forget her cute little chicken pox face, sitting on her favourite Teletubbies chair, hogging the TV. She was so cute. Now, she's one of my bestest friends and I tell her everything. She's literally a mini-me. Well, actually, we look the same age as well. She's gorgeous. I'm so lucky to have such an amazing brother and sister. The three of us have always been really close.

But yes, I can safely say, as first child I was a little bit spoilt, and I got all the attention from Nan and Granddad, plus all my other great nannies and granddads. If I look at the old family tapes now, all you can see is me singing, dancing, or just sitting still, being the centre of attention. They literally wanted every bit of movement on camera.

I've always been a little bit different when it comes to dressing up. From when I was tiny, I always wanted the shiniest version of something. If I was getting new shoes, they had to have a little bit of a heel on them. If I got new shoes from Clarks, I couldn't wait to show them off at school. I'd even roll up my skirt a bit just to be sure everyone got the full effect. Looking back, I'm not sure I always got quite the right look. Clarks school shoes are always pretty clumpy, and I've got really skinny legs, so most of the time, my feet just ended up looking absolutely massive. God, I must have looked like a right twat!

Even back to when I used to go to playgroup I used to kick up a fuss that I wanted to wear a dress. My mum would say, 'No, Megan, everyone will see your drawers, put on some shorts just so you can go and play,' and then she'd promise me I could put my dress on later, thinking I'd forget like any normal child would. But I never forgot a promise. If my mum said I could wear one later, I'd run home, demanding 'Where's my dress?' and the first thing I'd do was put that dress on.

My nan and granddad used to have a chalet in Sawbridgeworth in Hertfordshire, and that was our family's special spot. They lived there all summer with my granddad's mum Nanny Ginny, and Nanny Joan and Granddad Tom. They meant everything to me, and I was their little star. It was on the outskirts of the town, down a little path, right at the end, and it looked over a beautiful lake. We'd be there every single weekend and all the summer holidays. Our family were all friends with the neighbours, and they let us use their gate to get to the lake. That's where my granddad and I went to fish – our own little spot. Much later on down the track, I was sent to stay on a farm in Nashville for a TV show, and everyone saw me freaking out, but that was because of being made to stay in a pitch-black barn in the middle of nowhere. I was actually quite happy getting my hands dirty. All them years before at the chalet, if we weren't fishing, I used to help my granddad with his runner beans. Ha ha – what is this thing with runner beans and my family? Maybe that's why I use the word 'bean' so much. Do you call someone a bean if they do something stupid? I don't know, maybe it's just an Essex thing. To be honest, I actually think I'm a secret tomboy. The majority of my wardrobe is boy tracksuits, trucker hats and Nikes. Meanwhile, Nanny Ginny and Nanny Jean, used to sit in the white battered old chair. Nanny Ginny was chief peeler and Nanny Jean would be setting the table.

It was an amazing time in my life, and I have so many memories. As well as the chalet where mums and dads hung out, there was a caravan where all the kids slept. We had loads of toys, but we spent most of our time outside. We always got told to go and entertain ourselves somewhere. Proper country kids. One of our favourite ways to spend our time was to make our way to 'Beckingham Palace', as we and everyone else called it, just up the road. We'd stand by the gates for ages, waiting to see if Posh or Becks would drive through in a blacked-out car. It never happened, but we never gave up trying.

Even though I was this close every day to a proper Spice Girl, our favourite time was spent in the actual chalet. I loved it there – inside was really warm and cosy, full of ornaments, a tiny TV, and my nan's good luck horseshoes everywhere. Nan and Granddad's room was all peach-coloured, and the bathroom had these big suction mats. Me, my brother and sister were terrified there were spiders hiding underneath. Granddad smelled of kippers because he ate them all the time – he'd always put them with granary bread. Nanny Ginny would smother the bread with real butter, and my mum used to go mad, ha ha. Whenever I smell kippers now, it always takes me straight back to that special place. So many amazing memories. Really happy times!

The chalet was finally sold about ten years ago. It was really big, and by then, it was making too much work for my granddad, as there was a lot of land, so they sold up and moved to a bungalow in Chingford. But the chalet is where I had the real, best parts of my childhood. I'm not sure if it's actually legal, so I can't say whether this is true or not, but in 2016, when we lost my granddad, if we'd thought of it, we might have sprinkled his ashes, by the waterfall at the edge of the lake. As we all agreed at the time, there would have been no better place.

As well as my family, my other great love growing up was putting on a show. Even as a tiny tot, it was always me putting on a performance – singing, dancing, even a bit of acting. At Christmas, my favourite thing was to dress up as the Virgin Mary, and skip around in the hallway with a tea towel round my head, while all the relatives took turns to say, 'Well done, Megan.' I like to think I was actually quite good. No, hang on a minute, I WAS good!

Then it was off to Churchfields Juniors, my first school and the place I can 100 per cent say gave me the happiest years of my entire education. My brother and sister went there as well, so I still know quite a few people from them years, and I bump into them when I'm out and about locally. It feels like very few people have left the area.

I loved it at Churchfields. I had amazing friends, and when I said, 'Let's do a routine in the playground,' nobody ever refused. I was always really confident, even back then, and I'd always be breaking into song, but no matter what was going on, the signs that life wasn't going to be easy for me were there from the start. Like the time a bird shat on me mid-performance in the school playground. Sometimes, I'd even get out my violin and play a quick tune. Yes, you did read that correctly, ha ha. I know it's a bit random, I'm not really sure now why I wanted to do it, but I had violin lessons back then and even took up the piano for a bit as well. All them lessons and I can only play one song.

It's mad how the little things in my life used to make my day, like getting 20p for a slice of bread and butter, or carrot sticks. I used to queue up with my girls and then strut around the playground in my new Clarks shoes. If only life stayed that simple.

All I really wanted was to do something musical, even back then. I used to take my violin around Nanny Joan and Granddad Tom's house and play them tunes for hours at a time. How lucky they were to have a screeching violin in their ears every weekend! It probably sounded so bad, but bless them, they always sat and listened to everything really seriously, and then clapped really loudly at the end of every single tune.

Two other people who loved me performing and were always my biggest fans were Nanny Jean and my granddad. He's called Roy, but people called him Dick. Ha ha, what a nickname. He always told me, 'You're going to be a star, Megan.'

2

So far, so good, right? But let's not speak too soon,
because two massive things were about to happen to me.
They were completely separate, but they joined together
and ended up causing a lot of agg in my childhood. And
I would say they have really affected my whole life so far,
as you'll get to see. It was a horrible time for me, and, I'm
not going to lie, I really don't like talking about it, but I
want to be completely truthful about everything in my life.
Also, if me telling you what happened helps someone,
well then something good will have come out of it.
Anyway, here it goes...

When I was in Year Three at Churchfields, I began to
feel unwell. I was back and forth to the doctor, and they
said maybe I was allergic to something.

I kept having more and more tests to see what that might be. I started being sick and couldn't keep anything down. My parents were beside themselves, and all these doctors just kept scratching their heads. Eventually, my parents took me to see a homeopath, and she confirmed I was actually allergic to loads of stuff. Just to add to it, it was all my favourite foods, so it turned out I'd been eating loads of the wrong stuff my entire life.

They worked out I was allergic to wheat and gluten, and that was really, really sad for me because I loved my food. At that point my body had just said, 'Enough' and started to shut down. I wasn't actually diagnosed as having coeliac disease until about three years later – because all that time they weren't sure. When I was finally diagnosed with coeliac, it came after a whole extra load of hospital appointments and tests.

Coeliac disease is a really serious condition because it means your small intestine gets inflamed, so you can't absorb nutrients. It causes all sorts of problems like belly ache, diarrhoea and bloating. It can also make you feel really tired, because you're not getting enough energy from food, and keeps you really skinny. If you're not careful and don't follow a strict diet, you can end up with osteoporosis or even bowel cancer. Like I said, it's really serious, and, once you have it, it stays with you your whole life.

Once they knew what was wrong with me, I had to completely change my diet, and toughen up my immune system. I had a lot of time off school. That might sound like fun for a bit when you're eight, being at home and watching TV, but after a while it was terrible.

Because I was so ill, I didn't actually notice how bad it was at first. I was too busy being all frail, pale and really, really skinny. It was only as I started to get better that I began to notice how much I was missing out on. I can remember now, I was soooo bored! Milly was still a baby, Harry was at school by then, so guess who I had for company? Bratz dolls! Dunno if you ever played with Bratz dolls, but my favourite was Yasmin. She was tanned with brown hair, and I wanted to look like her. By then, I was too old to be playing with dolls, but because I was at home a lot, there wasn't much else to do – it was just me and my Bratz.

Yep, I remember it now, total nightmare, but the time did finally pass – I got a bit better and I was allowed to go back to school. It was great being back with my mates and all the other kids, but I still had to be extra careful, which wasn't much fun. I was always that 'sick kid' at school. There's always one, isn't there? Well, at my school, I was that 'one'. If a bug was going round, I definitely caught it! So then I had to have time off again.

Nothing lasts forever, though, and I did get a bit stronger during those last couple of years at Churchfields. I was on a really strict diet, and everyone actually got a bit jealous because I was allowed to eat special food that my mum made me. She even used to bring me in takeaways.

So I can definitely say that my bad health didn't knock my confidence at all when it was my only problem. Things only started going really bad for me when I had to leave Churchfields and go to secondary school. That meant going to Woodbridge, stepping into the complete unknown, and, trust me, I was absolutely shitting myself.

3

I know changing schools isn't that big a deal. Everyone does it, and has that thing of making new friends and learning the ropes again. But Woodbridge was massive in comparison with my old school, so while lots of Churchfields people went along, it turned out none of my old friends were in my class. It was full of kids from other places, and most of them already seemed to know each other. At this point in my life, I became very shy – I know that may sound hard to believe – and I'd say I didn't really stand out at all. Except when I did grab people's attention, and it wasn't in a good way!

I still had all my allergies, which meant I had to bring my lunch food in a little box. Plus, I'd had to have train tracks fitted onto my teeth literally the month before I started secondary school. The timing for that couldn't have been worse! I had a bit of an overbite as well, so every night I was in a neck brace to try to correct it. Not exactly glamorous, ha ha.

My braces were pink, and one night I ate spaghetti Bolognese and they got stained orange. I had to go to school looking like that, and that didn't exactly help my confidence. Another time, I was swinging on my chair in class. Pretty normal, except somehow I managed to fall through the chair – I hit my jaw on the table, so that my teeth AND tracks went through my lip. Blood went everywhere! I've actually had so much lip filler these days, you can't really see the scar any more, but for a while it was bad – this massive purple bruise coming out of my mouth. When the braces finally came off, I had to wear a retainer for a bit with a false tooth. I was in those train tracks for a year, and, trust me, it was a very, very long year.

So I had all these things wrong with me, and let's just say they didn't exactly help me fit in at Woodbridge.

I do want to make it clear there were some nice people at that school. There was this little group I joined in the music club at lunchtime. I could take my violin there and have lessons or just practise in the room. I was the youngest one, and there were some nice boys and girls up there, all a bit different from the usual, doing their own thing like singing and playing instruments. Basically, we had our own little glee club in Essex.

That music room was a little getaway for me, and there was a really nice music teacher called Mrs Wright. But everywhere else was becoming a nightmare. It was just one of them things. My year at Woodbridge could have been a nice bunch of kids, but it just happened to be a vile one. I knew a few girls from Churchfields, but they found a new crowd, and they were all a bit bitchy. The ones I already knew were never bitchy to me before, but they turned and started being not very nice.

I've always been someone who, if someone's being picked on, I make a big effort so they get included. There was a nice girl with learning difficulties. She'd also been at Churchfields, where she'd had people looking out for her. Now, I sat next to her and tried to help her, but the people around us were just horrible. My class wasn't even that bad, I just didn't know anyone that well. The boys thought they were gangsters, and the girls all behaved like rude girls. I ended up thinking they were all scum, just a bunch of bullies.

In Year Seven, a boy asked me to the school dance. I said 'No,' but the next thing I knew, I was getting a phone call from some girl. It was all, 'Don't you dare go to the dance with him, he's talking to one of my mates.' I wasn't even interested in him and I barely knew the girl he was apparently talking to, but what could I do? He'd asked me, but without even trying, I'd ended up in some psycho-drama and from that moment, they wouldn't leave me alone. Then I sang in a school show, and from that moment on, the bullying really started.

That single school year, Year Seven, was one of the worst of my life. Woodbridge is divided into two big main buildings, Mallards and Wynndale, and you have to walk down a lane between them to get to lessons. Every time I had to do it, it felt like the longest walk of my life. I had a few incidents, and, in one of them, a girl spat in my face. I was so scared to report it, and at that time, I was worried these girls would come and find me, but now, looking back, I'm glad I did report it. I remember having to flick through the school yearbook pages looking for the girl who did it.

It never stopped. I had these shoes with a little kitten heel on them – I've always liked to be a bit different – but people would laugh at them, taking the piss out of them for no real reason. Then, one day in the corridor, these same bullies were there, which just made me really nervous, and I ended up falling down the stairs as I tried to get past them. They all laughed, and even while I was picking myself up, I could feel myself boiling up. I just thought, 'Someone's fallen down the stairs and you're laughing. Really?' It just showed their values – it was all about being in a group. It was more cool to act cool, and not help. It gets me fuming even now just remembering it. No more kitten heels after that. Don't get me wrong, I wouldn't even wear kitten heels now, but back in the day, I thought they were fashionable.

The worst thing was what happened to my diet. I still had all these stomach problems, but it felt like my little lunch box made me an easy target. To try to fit in better with everyone, I even stopped following my special diet. How bad is that? I was just trying to be normal, wanting to go to the lunch hall and queue up with everyone else. I would have done anything not to stand out and to avoid being picked on. That's how powerful them bullies are! They make you do stuff where you end up damaging yourself.

By now, I was taking Nurofen and paracetamol every day. I got to a point where I was so ill that my mum said, 'That's enough, you're not eating that food any more,' and she started making me chicken salads. I felt really isolated – I didn't have a lot of friends anyway, and everyone was either in the cool group, or trying to get in it. I ended up so unhappy that they started giving me counselling sessions. I'll say this – the school did what it could. The counsellors asked me, 'Who would you like to come to your next session?' so that I could maybe start a new group of friends. There was a girl called Ghurdeep who I liked, and also Laura, Shellie, Robyn and Georgia from my old school, so I recruited them. I had a few lessons where I tried to stick with them, but those other girls carried on being so nasty, it didn't give me enough protection from the bullies.

I was walking along the corridor with my friend Laura one day, and this girl who everyone was scared of came up to us. She'd been threatening to beat me up if I went to the dance with that boy who asked me. This girl ended up smacking Laura around the face. Laura was tall, I was little and she started screaming at both of us. I couldn't do anything – instead I just stood there petrified. My friends were nice girls, but in situations like these, they couldn't stand up for themselves either. The counsellors tried to help me focus on the positive, but it was a terrible situation.

After this girl threatened to beat me up, I came out of school for a few days. Then my mum came in with me to speak to the head, asking why they'd allowed it to happen and what they were going to do about it. The teachers all said I would be okay, nothing would happen, but then I started to worry because my mum had come in. And shock, rumours started that my mum was coming in to beat up one of the other girls. So that just made it all worse. My poor mum was just being there for me.

One day soon after that, I was walking through the playground and it literally felt like I'd been smashed in the back of my head. I fell to the floor, and it took me a while to realise I'd been smacked from behind with a wet inner sole of a shoe, by a boy in my class. Once I was on the ground, everyone crowded round and he continued to slap me. Someone videoed the whole thing. Turned out I was the latest victim of 'happy slapping'. I'll never forget lying on the floor, drenched in a puddle of water. My friends were shouting at this boy, not knowing what to do while he kept slapping me about seven times. Eventually some older girls ran out and pulled him off, but by then I was hysterical. It became a serious incident at the school – the head said anybody caught with the video on their phone would be instantly excluded, so the film got deleted.

It might not sound like much, but something that hurt me nearly as bad was when one of the girls spread a rumour that I had nits. In the scheme of things, it's not actually that bad, but it's the worst thing to go round a school when you're that age. I didn't want to go to school any more. I started trying to avoid going in, I stopped playing violin, I stopped singing – I thought giving everything up might help me fit in, but nothing worked. I always sat next to the girl who had learning difficulties, because she had carers nearby, and I hoped they would protect me. I turned into a shy, weak, quiet child, scared all the time, waiting for the next bad thing.

I also became really skinny again, and the teachers had a note from my mum which said, 'Megan suffers from migraines, so when she needs her tablets, please let her go.' That note, which only the teachers knew about, was actually so I could go to the toilet, because by then, I had all my belly problems back again. I was such a nervous wreck, I needed to go to the toilet the whole time.

I was so skinny, my arms became hairy, so of course one boy pointed this out to the rest of the class. 'Why are your arms so hairy? People that have hairy arms like that are anorexic.' Lovely. For the rest of the summer, I used to sit in my blazer, sweating so bad but not taking it off, just so I could avoid any more comments.

I was just coeliac and I had allergies, but because of all the comments, I wasn't eating what I was supposed to. I even started hating science lessons, not because I didn't like science, but because science meant putting my hair up, and putting my hair up meant having my ears on show. This probably wouldn't affect any other person, but some of the boys in my class said I had elf ears, and all these little comments just got to me. So I'd do anything to avoid it.

By now, my confidence was so low, I used to go and eat my lunch on my own in the stairwell, because I didn't want people to see me get food caught in my train tracks. I didn't want them to see my salad – too different. One day, I was feeling miserable like always, and I remember standing there, thinking, 'I don't want to be at this school any more, I hate my life.'

Finally, someone thought it would be hilarious to steal my door keys. I had a Playboy key ring, and someone – let's call her BB – stole it when I was in the music room.

My parents were worried this would mean someone could break in, so they had to get all the locks on our house changed. Soon after, one of my coloured keys got found underneath the piano where it had been put back.

Almost at the same time, I had a tiny little mobile phone, and an unknown caller rang it. A girl's voice said, 'When you come out tomorrow night, I'm going to get you stabbed.' I put the phone down, shaking.

I thought I recognised a girl's voice in the background, and my dad drove me round to her house. Turned out it was the girl's cousin who'd phoned me. That was the last straw for my parents, and they pulled me out of school.

I didn't even bother telling anyone I'd left, I was just so glad to be gone. It had always been my dream to go to theatre school. My nan and granddad, always a massive part of my life, had saved up enough money and used their savings to send me, as my mum and dad couldn't afford to.

A couple of weeks in, I was coming back from my new theatre school. I was walking back from the station in my new uniform, and it had 'private school girl' written all over it – bright green and white stripes like a deckchair, emerald green blazer with a gold trim, the works. I was happy – until me and my mates walked past a crowd from Woodbridge, and they all kicked off saying stuff about my uniform. By now, I'd got away from them, but their words still really got to me. I'd heard through the grapevine that these same girls were saying loads of mean stuff like, 'Megan thinks she's better than everyone else because she goes to theatre school. Who does she think she is?' So when I was at their school, they picked on me. And when I left, they picked on me. WTF? I just couldn't win.

I felt weak, and I was frightened that other people I hardly knew had so much power over me. These girls were the ones everyone liked or fancied, and I was a nobody. They were mean girls; I was brace-face. When I first came across them, of course I wanted to be in their crowd as well, but it got so awful, I went from admiring them to hating them. I was looking in my diary from that time recently, and one girl's name kept popping out of the page. I can't actually remember any one thing she did, but her name kept appearing, so I'm guessing she must have been one of them who hurt me the most. Isn't it crazy to think I don't even know now what this girl done to me, but her name got written down so many times in my diary, she must have done me a lot of damage.

I'd love to be able to say I've forgiven them for what they did, but I don't know if I'll ever be able to do that. I was a happy kid and they destroyed a year of my life just to look cool. I'm still a local girl, so I do still bump into those same faces from time to time. Whenever I see them now, I act as if I don't even know them, and I feel quite good about myself, because I used to look at them and think, 'Why can't I be like you? I want everyone to fancy me too,' and now I see them and it's clear time has not been kind. I must admit, I did have a smile on my face when I drove past one of them in my lovely white Range Rover, my dream car since I was a kid. Their lives haven't moved on – they're still hanging out in the same places they always did, while I've just built my first home with my own money. If they were to ask me how I was, I'd say, 'Great, how are you?' and I'd want them to know I'm doing something I love. To be honest, my happiness is probably the best punishment for them, but it doesn't make it okay. Them memories will always be with me. Them girls will probably have no idea the effect they had on me, but they need to realise what they put me through, and probably other people too after I left school.

It's a big part of me, and I think it's always going to stay with me. Last year, I had therapy because I felt I couldn't control my anger, and it definitely all stems from that time. It's definitely damaged me a little bit. All these years later – you've seen it enough on telly to know – the tiniest thing can set me off, because it immediately brings back all the feelings I had in that stairwell, in that lane between the schools, on the ground in the playground. If two girls are whispering, they might not even be talking about me, but I'll immediately think they are, or I'll assume they might be planning to do something hurtful.

Sometimes I'll think it's safer just to believe the worst. Doesn't exactly make me the most relaxed person.

I worry that people just see that side of me and get me all wrong. If you were to listen back to some of them arguments I've had on TV in the past, but instead heard them inside my head, you'd know they always come from a good place. I just want everyone to be heard and to be treated fairly. The reason it goes so wrong is because of how I express myself. I can't control my emotions because the anger takes over, and that's always been my downfall.

Bullying is vile. People have seen me lose my shit on the telly over and over again, and they probably assume I'm the bully, because I shout and use swear words, but I never could be, because of what I went through myself. In fact, a lot of me losing it with people and not being able to control my temper comes from how I was treated. I was always the quiet one, I was always too scared to speak up, so now I'm probably just trying to make up for it!

For as long as I can remember, it was my dream to go to theatre school. I'd seen all them films full of girls hanging out in dance studios – breaking into song in the canteen, you know the sort – and I wanted to be exactly like one of them girls with the leotard, legwarmers, the works. During my time at Churchfields and Woodbridge, I went to a Saturday school in Chigwell called Stage Coach – this is what would get me through the week and I can truly say it helped with my confidence. The owner, Suzanna, was amazing and I thank her now for that. But now I didn't have to worry about the bullies, I could chase my dream – just like in the films.

My mum arranged for me to have an audition at the Ravenscourt Theatre School in Hammersmith, West

London. This was for full-time theatre school #BigDeal. The lady who ran it was Roe Brooks – one of her old pupils was her own daughter, Charlie, who became famous as Janine in *EastEnders*. The school used to be called Corona School, and all sorts of big names went there, from actors like Patsy Kensit, Nicholas Lyndhurst and Dennis Waterman, to soap stars like Dean Gaffney and Helen Worth from *Corrie*. I'd never wanted anything so badly in my life. They asked me to sing and do a monologue, and they told me straight away I was in.

When the letter came confirming that I'd been accepted, I was so excited I couldn't believe it, especially when my nan and granddad said they would help pay my fees to go. Also, my Nanny Ginny had passed away by then, and she'd left all her grandkids a bit of money. I used this money to buy my tap shoes, ballet shoes, school books and everything else. Ravenscourt was proper posh. My mum and I had to go up to Harrods to buy the uniform – it cost a fortune, unsurprisingly, but my mum and dad managed to scrape together some more pennies for it. Like I said earlier, it was bright green, so I stood out like a sore thumb on the train platform at Woodford each morning, but that was all right, I liked it. Bye-bye Woodbridge, hello dream.

I always knew I wanted to be a singer and work in musicals, but, not gonna lie, even then I knew I wanted to be a solo superstar. From when I was really little, I loved

Britney Spears and Christina Aguilera – I listened to them constantly, and I loved the fact they were such massive stars. My favourite song for ages was 'I'm Not a Girl' by Britney.

By the time I got to Ravenscourt, I was in love with Miley Cyrus. Anybody who asked, I said, 'I want to be the next Hannah Montana.' I wanted to follow in her footsteps and be on the Disney Channel and perform all over the world. When I was in art class, I'd design all the stage plans for my world tour, LOL. My dream was to spend at least half my working life on a big tour bus. I didn't even know country music existed back then, but I was always writing down lyrics whenever they came into my head.

Everybody knew this was what I wanted to do. In my singing lessons, in front of everyone, my teacher started playing 'When Will I Be Famous' by Bros as soon as I walked into the room. I used to love it, and I loved my singing teacher, Mr Dawes. He brought all my confidence back.

At Woodbridge, I'd be dreading every minute of the day from the moment I woke up in the morning. Now, every day became really long and intense, but in a good way. School started at 8.30am, which meant we all had to be there for about 8.15. Ravenscourt is on the other side of London from my parents' house, though, which meant I had to be out of the house by seven

o'clock every morning. There happened to be a group
of us coming from Essex in my year – Chloe Meadows
was one of them – and we all used to travel into town
together every day. Every single day we never quite
made it for 8.15, and every single day the lady on school
reception would shout 'Late again, Essex,' as we ran
through. We'd all fib and say there'd been delays on the
train, but actually it was because we'd stopped off in
Hammersmith for a McDonald's breakfast. Good times.
It was 1 hour 15 minutes there, 1 hour 15 minutes home.
That's commitment!

Ravenscourt was like a normal school in the mornings
– all books and boring stuff. Then, at one o'clock, we had
lunch and got changed. From then on, it was singing,
dancing, acting, everything I'd wanted to do, until four
o'clock. It was really full on, especially if I had a private
lesson afterwards, which meant I got home around 7.30pm
every night. Then I'd start all over again the next day. And
guess what? After all those sick days at Woodbridge, I
didn't miss a single day at Ravenscourt. I used to go to
bed so excited for the next day.

I could bring my special food in, and the school's chef
would heat it up, so my health got better, even though I
was putting my body through loads more physical stress
with all the dancing. In fact, I'd say everything got better.

There were no bullies there, just lots of nice new friends, all there for the same reason as me. Being there really helped my confidence.

There was a talent agency linked to the school, and through them, I got my first ever job. Wait for it... a Hannah Montana advert! That was how I found out I loved Miley so much. I got so obsessed.

I never got to meet Miley or anything, but it set me on the right path and, from then on, I was always up to something. I was a Quidditch player for Gryffindor in one of the *Harry Potter* movies, so I got to meet them all. I even spoke to Daniel Radcliffe, and wished him a Happy Valentine's Day. I turned up in everything from the Disney Channel to documentaries on Channel 4. I was always popping up somewhere on TV. Whenever I was due on screen, my family would all gather round the telly, and see who could spot me first.

Don't get me wrong, it wasn't easy from then on. I had more than my share of rejections, plenty of turnaways from auditions and loads more noes than yeses along the way. I went for my first ever audition when I was ten, for *Chitty Chitty Bang Bang* at the London Palladium, and I got to the last stages. I was word-perfect, but somehow I messed up one line when I was in the room, and that was it, all over. I was gutted, but it didn't stop me. Rejection was hard, still is, but you get used to it. I walked out one time, and another girl was crying in front of me. I mean, really sobbing! I remember watching her and thinking even then, 'It's fine, there'll be others, I'll get something.' Not everyone had the same mind set as me, but I always knew what I wanted, and I had enough positive people on my side to encourage me. My granddad always told me, 'You're going to make it,' and I believed him.

It wasn't just me who got involved in it all, though. My mum got used to getting in the car on a Saturday morning and driving me miles away – all part of my mission to make myself a star. I bought *The Stage* magazine every week, and we religiously went through all the ads for likely auditions. I don't know what I would have done without my mum. After working all week, she'd spend her weekends driving little Megan to places like Birmingham and Bournemouth so she could sing her little heart out.

One of the biggest series of auditions each year was always for *The X Factor*. One year, the auditions took place at London's ExCeL, and we got ourselves really organised.

We even took our own tent and camped out overnight in the car park in Docklands, next to the arena where the auditions were taking place. By now, we were proper audition veterans, so when we arrived the evening before, we carefully worked out where to pitch the tent so we'd be nearest the door in the morning and get a decent spot in the queue. We'd only just set an early alarm and put our heads down in our sleeping bags when we heard loads of people rushing about outside. My mum stuck her head out the tent to see what was going on, and just then we heard someone shout, 'They've changed the door!' It was an absolute nightmare as hundreds of people went mad grabbing all their stuff – pillows, mattresses, bags of makeup, costumes, tents – and we all started running towards the other corner of the car park. And, after all that drama, I still didn't get through. I was absolutely gutted, but now, when I look back on it, I gotta laugh. Sometimes it turns out you have to quite literally chase the dream!

My tips for following your dream

💋 Don't worry about what other people are doing

💋 Either be the first, or be different #Nashvilleinspo

💋 No matter how well you're doing, don't take it for granted

💋 Never forget, the harder you work, the luckier you'll get

💋 Remember that for every hundred Noes, you only need one Yes

💋 Always remember that your mum is always right #tipforlife #listentoTanya

NEVER GIVE UP!

5

I've got hundreds of good memories from all those
auditions – meeting people, hanging out, having a laugh
with my mum – but unfortunately, I do also have one
massively dodgy episode to report, and I hope it serves as
a warning to all those young girls just like me, willing to do
anything to get a break.

I'd found a talent agency on the internet, and it had
links to loads of auditions all over the UK. I sent off my
show reel, and a woman called Fran emailed me to say
I'd made the shortlist over thousands of other girls. She
even asked me to contact her within twenty-four hours
to arrange an audition. It all sounded really promising,
especially when she said she'd introduce me to a music
producer called James. Apparently, he was a producer for

Def Jam, a massive US record label, but he'd heard my demo and was now deciding whether to work with me or one other girl on an album. Two days later, I was on my way to a hotel in Bristol to meet James. Don't worry, my mum came along with me and it all seemed above board. Famous last words...

We found James on his own in the hotel bar, but he said one of his team was working upstairs, while the rest of them were 'busy in the studio working with Labrinth'. Pretty impressive. James then sat with me and my mum for FOUR HOURS, telling us in detail everything he knew about the music industry and all the amazing things he'd done. He told us exactly how my voice would fit into all these projects he had going on. He even called my old agent and other people I'd been working for. At one point, he was even talking about whether he could buy the rights to a song I'd already recorded. Pretty thorough, I'll give him that! It was all very impressive, and we fell for it.

Finally, he told us, he'd decided to go with me over the other girl. He told me he'd be putting a £70,000 advance into my bank account for the album, that I'd be flying out to America the very next week, and that I'd be living in one of his record company's apartments for the next five months while we made the album. Not only that, but we'd be recording the first track the very next day. Amazing! It all sounded too good to be true.

There was one moment that seemed a bit dodgy – he came up to me and out of the blue said, 'Were you lying about not having a boyfriend?' I'd been seeing someone, but I was single at that point so that's what I said. James added, 'I've found out you've got a boyfriend in your home town.' WTF? He was being jokey, not aggressive, but at the time I didn't know how James would even know about my nearly-boyfriend. I just figured they were investing a whole load of money in me, so it made sense they'd do some digging. Anyway...

James had dinner with me and my mum, but he kept saying we needed to get back to the hotel to write the first song I'd be recording. At this point, James kindly pointed out to my mum that she needed to go home and get my old agency contracts, passport and other official paperwork, otherwise he wouldn't be able to work with me the next day! Yes, the warning lights should have gone on at this point, but he said he'd booked me a separate hotel room, so I could get an early night and rest my voice. He spoke about everything in such detail, it all seemed above board, and so my mum planned to drive back to Essex, collect the contracts and come straight back.

Meanwhile, back at the hotel, I wanted to get a good night's sleep. It was all getting very late, and James and I got in the lift to go to our rooms. I put out my hand for my door key, but just then he mentioned there was a problem with my room, so we'd have to wait in his room for a while.

He said we could write the song while we waited. Okay then... I sat, while he asked me loads of questions so he could 'base the lyrics on my life'. It was all weird stuff, like...

'What's your relationship like with your family?'

'Really good, thanks.'

'What do you dream of doing with your life?'

'Singing, performing, making records.'

'What would you do if a guy who was a millionaire came up to you with your career in his hands and said "Fuck me"?'

I sat there and froze. I'm already a paranoid person, I over-think about everything, and it suddenly hit me – 'This isn't right.' How could someone go from normal to weird in seconds?

At this point, I made a quick call to my mum to find out where she was. I knew she was coming back, but I told her to phone me in an hour and check in on me.

He didn't like that much. 'You should have a bit more independence, Megan,' he said. Then it was, 'No more phones. We're working!'

From then on, it got more and more awkward between the two of us as he asked me loads more dark questions – 'Have you been sexually abused?' and 'If a guy was ugly but had loads of money, would you fuck him?' Not only that, but he started making all these trips to the bathroom, in between running his hands through his hair, walking around the room and occasionally touching himself in a suggestive way. At this point, I was planning my escape, especially after I noticed his suitcase on the bed had nothing but papers in it, and there was a pair of tracksuit bottoms on the floor – not exactly what a high-powered music exec would be wearing. All these messed-up thoughts started to go through my head. 'This guy isn't who he says he is. So who is he, and how am I going to get out of here?'

At this point, he switched the subject to himself, saying how he'd paid a famous porn star £250,000 to teach him all the moves to 'make a girl squirt'. He told me how many girls he'd slept with, how good he was in bed, that I seemed like a snob – oh, and that his dad had cancer, his mum was dead and his sister had committed suicide by jumping off a cliff. Can you imagine? Then he said he'd been told he had twelve months to live, and that he'd actually been told that six months ago. For that last bit, I managed to say, 'I'm sorry.' But for the rest, I just sat in silence. I was terrified.

Finally, he called someone about my room, and guess what? It turned out there wasn't one. The hotel had messed up the booking. He said to me, 'Don't worry, I've asked them to bring a spare bed up to my room.'

I have to admit, I was shaking with nerves by now, but I somehow managed to find my voice – I told him he was making me very uncomfortable, and that I needed my own room. This seemed to make him annoyed, and he

replied, 'Oh right, yeah, I was going to get you your
own room, anyway.'

You're probably thinking, 'Why is this girl not just
running out?' But I was scared. I knew I was going to get
out, but I didn't want to rile him up, so I was going with the
flow for now and planning my escape.

James disappeared for a bit, and I was sat on the bed,
thinking, 'How am I going to get out of here?' I was looking
at the door, and I suddenly saw the peephole change
colour, as if he had been standing outside the room the
whole time, clearly not sorting out this room thing.

I sat completely still, holding on to my bags, and
wondering how on earth I was going to get out of this
hell-hole situation without pissing him off even more. But
it was getting worse for me, especially when James came
back and suddenly announced that the entire hotel was
full but he'd somehow sorted me out a suite. He gave me
the key, so I went upstairs to this new room while he went
downstairs. The first thing I saw in the suite was a bottle
of wine and two glasses set out. This was not happening! I
instantly called my mum, and told her I didn't feel safe, but
I had no idea what to do. She tried to calm me down, but I
was starting to shake. She said she was on her way back
and she'd call me again in twenty minutes.

Then James turned up back at the suite, but I think
by then he'd finally realised how scared I was of him. He
insisted on using my phone and used it to book a room

for me at another hotel. He said his friend would pick me up, but I wasn't having it. I said I'd get a cab, but instead he insisted on walking me. That was a nightmare in itself, him taking me down all these back alleys when we could have just walked along the main road. He asked again for my phone so he could type his email address into it, and it was then I caught a glimpse of his phone. On the screen, I saw 'SOS' and 'SIM not recognised'. All that time, he'd pretended to be talking to people, but he couldn't actually make one call!

He'd taken my phone to use, but instead he'd been going down all my messages, and he saw all the texts I'd sent my mum while he had me held up in his hotel room. This set him off again. 'I can't believe you're so ungrateful and selfish, after everything I've done for you today, giving you this opportunity, and you're texting your mum telling her you're uncomfortable.'

I tried to keep calm and just kept saying how sorry I was, but by now he was giving me the silent treatment, so we just stood there awkwardly – him sulking, me shaking, until after a bit he let me walk the rest of the route to the hotel on my own. I've never felt so relieved to be on my own, getting to that hotel. Before I walked away, he said, 'Make sure you say it's for Fran.' I found it really weird, but I was just happy to get away from him.

I called my mum, who was already on her way back from Essex to Bristol, and she told me to change rooms, so I did – and I asked the receptionist not to give anyone else a key. An hour later – by now it was three o'clock in the morning – I received an email from James: 'U ok? Meet me at 9, don't worry about saying thank you LOL.' This guy seriously thought he still had me in the palm of his hand. What he didn't realise was, my mum was coming to pick me up and take me straight home.

Bless her, my mum got even less sleep than me that night. As soon as she'd got my first call, she'd phoned reception at the hotel where I was with James – he'd told us it was fully booked and they told her there were actually loads of rooms available. So that was just another lie James told us. At that point, she was about an hour from home in Essex, but she turned the car round as soon as she got my call and headed back to Bristol, staying in touch with me by phone the whole way. I was in shock about the whole thing – it was only when my mum finally appeared that I burst into tears. We tried to get some sleep, but we were both so messed up in the head, we probably only got half an hour between us. By seven o'clock the next morning, we were back on the road home, and we reported it to the police, just so they had something on file in case James tried to do this to anybody else.

Once I was safe back in Essex, I emailed James asking for more details about him and his record company, but he refused to send me any info. Instead, 'Fran' had started emailing me as soon as I'd left Bristol. Hmmm. It was weird that I never heard from her the whole time I spent with 'James'. Could it be they were actually the same person?

My mum contacted someone at Def Jam. It turned out James didn't exist.

I received a couple of strange calls too, from a boy called 'John'. Could that be him as well? But now I was safe back in Woodford, I just blocked his number and got on with my life.

One day soon after, on the talent agency account where all the trouble had started, I received an email from – guess who? 'Fran'. Telling me I'd made the shortlist over thousands of other girls and asking me to get back to them within the next twenty-four hours to arrange an audition. I didn't reply.

What's terrifying about this story is how easy it is for people to take advantage of young, innocent girls who want to make it, who probably aren't as clued up as me, but are equally hungry, just because they're desperate to get their big break. It doesn't matter if they're promising a modelling contract or a debut album – that 'James' story shows how easy it is for arseholes to make false promises when actually all they want to do is take advantage of young girls.

My mum and I had both been to hundreds of auditions by then and spoken to all sorts of people in the industry. But all that didn't matter – we both still got fooled by

James, with his really smooth manner and how much he seemed to know about the music industry. I was young, hungry and very naïve, so to him I was probably just an easy target.

He was incredibly convincing when my mum was there, but he turned into somebody completely different as soon as she went. Even though it pissed him off that I stayed in contact with my mum all night, he knew he wouldn't be able to get away with anything. But to anyone else, something terrible could have happened. So I just want to say this to all of you out there. Please take note – if something sounds too good to be true, I hate to tell you, but it probably is.

6

God, doesn't my life sound depressing right now? Ha ha. Sorry about that. Let me tell you a happier story... Hmmm... Oh, I know... I'm going to tell you all about me and *Britain's Got Talent.*

I'll be honest, it was all a bit random. It was near the end of my third year at Ravenscourt and my exams were around the corner, but I was still doing loads of tryouts. Then a girl from the year below me called Demi said we should audition for *BGT*. As you do.

It was 2009 – this was the third series. We all knew about the first winner, Paul Potts, back in 2007, but the show wasn't that big back then. But my year turned out to be massive. Demi and I happened to enter at the same time as a group called Diversity and a singer called Susan Boyle.

Well, Demi and I got together and started rehearsing as a duet. We called ourselves Harmony and dressed ourselves up in tutus, for some reason I'll never really know. I used to be able to do the splits so that became part of our routine as well. It was probably one of the most over-the-top performances of my entire life – we'd raided Primark the night before and picked every single pair of neon legwarmers, neon headbands and tutus we could get our hands on.

My heart sank when we turned up for the first round of auditions in a hall in central London. Once again, there were queues around the block – thousands of people all waiting in the freezing cold. Demi and I got through that first round and then all the other early stages you don't even see on the telly. There are actually loads of rounds, before the TV shows, that the viewers never get to hear about. By the time we were finally on stage in front of Simon Cowell, Amanda Holden and Piers Morgan, we'd already made a video and done loads of other stuff so we were well up for it.

Because of all those other auditions, it hadn't occurred to me for a minute that Harmony would actually get through, so I was pretty terrified when we found ourselves on stage with the cameras facing us as well as the judges. We performed a song from the musical *Wicked* called 'What Is This Feeling?' – Piers was really nice, Amanda showered us with praise, and Simon said he hated the song but liked us. So that made three yeses, and we were through to the live shows.

At that point, it all got a bit serious. You name it, we got it – professional help, dance lessons, vocal training, the works. The best bit was getting to choose our outfits. These were designed by top pros, the same people who make outfits for *Dancing on Ice*. I have to say, though, all that expert advice was probably what ended up getting us in a muddle when it came to choosing our music. We were originally meant to do a version of 'The Climb' by – who else – Miley Cyrus, but then 'they' decided we needed something more upbeat, so then it was going to be something by Abba, and then 'they' changed their minds again. Finally, they settled on 'Girls Just Wanna Have Fun' by Cyndi Lauper. That meant we had to learn a really upbeat dance routine, with both Demi and myself dressed in bright pink leotards, and the plan was for us to jump out of a cake at the beginning. Hmm... Well, I'm not sure if I mentioned it earlier, but I have a few food allergies. I know, I know, I don't like to go on about it, ha ha. Well, unfortunately, my allergies meant the cake had to be made of... mashed potato! For one of the biggest parts of the routine, we had to have a massive food fight on stage, and all I can remember is mashed potato ending up going everywhere. Ant and Dec had to step over it all when they came on stage at the end.

But it turned out we hadn't done enough to impress the judges. Piers and Amanda were nice about us again, but Simon had had enough of us. He said, 'I thought everything was great, other than the singing. The singing was sort of atrocious, but then the Spice Girls were number one.'

When it got to the results coming in, I remember standing on stage, holding Demi's hand, just wishing we'd get through. Once again, this was another stage of my life when I just wanted to make it, but it turned out to all end there.

We didn't really have a chance when the public's favourites were Susan Boyle and Diversity. I do believe the producers have an idea from the start of who they want to promote to the end. During our round, we were up against Stavros Flatley, and they'd already become a favourite and were getting loads of screen time and mentions in the press, unlike us. Susan Boyle was also there that day, doing press interviews even though she wasn't scheduled to perform, and right then, I knew they had it all planned – she was going to be their breakout star.

From my perspective, I wouldn't say *BGT* is fixed, but I would say the producers know exactly who they want to win, and they do their best to make it happen. But that's show business.

I'm not going to lie, appearing on *Britain's Got Talent* didn't exactly change my life. Demi and I did some interviews, and we got recognised a few times afterwards, especially if we were together – 'Were you the girls who jumped out of the cake?' One day we were leaving the GMTV studio, and a pap took a photo of us. You're supposed to play it cool when that happens, but I was so excited I ran down to the gates and shouted, 'There's a photographer!' just in case he missed us, and I posed for pictures.

At the same time as we left *BGT,* I left Ravenscourt and was on summer break before my next school. I filled the break by going on the road with Harmony. We stayed in tiny hotels along the way and we had to rehearse in a church hall in Huddersfield, but as far as I was concerned, we'd hit the big time. We even had a manager, a really geeky guy called Chris. Okay, so we didn't have to work that hard to get him, he'd basically emailed both our mums and offered his services, but hey... He gave us a song called 'Party Time', which was possibly the worst song ever, all about having a party, jumping on clouds and arriving at a castle in the sky. We made a video to go with it, wearing prom dresses and filming at Demi's school. Low budget is probably pretty accurate.

As part of our 'tour', Demi and I went to about six different schools and performed for the pupils in the assembly halls. We did it in our special outfits but I have to say it was still a bit amateur. God knows what those kids must have thought, turning up for assembly one morning, expecting to get a hymn and instead finding us two jumping up and down in our pink leotards and tutus. We also turned up wherever a region was doing their own version of ...*Got Talent,* and Demi and I were meant to be the guest stars. Sometimes we even got a red carpet. Hilarious.

Is it fair to say I'd hit the big time? Possibly not. But even though I was only in Huddersfield, at that time for me it could have been LA. Our minibus might not have been my dream tour bus, but you've got to start somewhere.

Is it time to talk about boys? Probably. Well, if you believe everything you read in the press, apparently I'm in and out of relationships every time the wind changes, but the truth is, I've actually only had a handful of boyfriends, and even fewer who I would say I've actually loved. When it comes to that, it's definitely fair to say that when I do fall for someone, I give my all to the relationship, sometimes even when it has ended up costing me my own feelings. But I don't see the point of going into something half-hearted. I just wish I'd loved myself a bit more sometimes. But we live and learn, right?

The first boys I used to fancy at primary school were Jason White and Miles Brett. Jason is still one of me and my brother's friends to this day, but he was the boy at

above and below: **Me as a baby with (*clockwise*) Mum (Tanya), Dad (Dave) and Granddad**

above: **My first home in South Woodford**

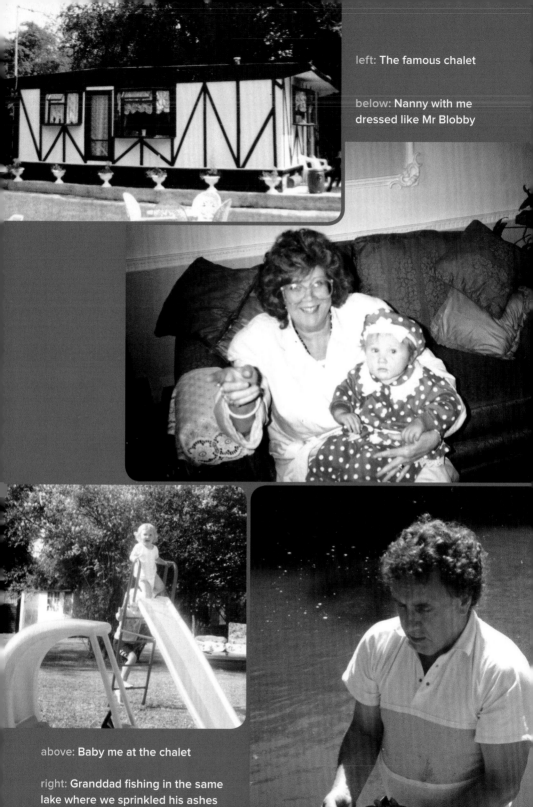

left: The famous chalet

below: Nanny with me dressed like Mr Blobby

above: Baby me at the chalet

right: Granddad fishing in the same lake where we sprinkled his ashes

left: Me down the chalet with Granddad and Nanny Ginny

below: Baby Harry with me in my favourite Esmeralda PJs

right: Performing to my nannies in the living room

above: **Me, Harry and Milly aged six, four and one**

right: **Party streamers, aged eight**

below: **Family photo (rocking the small hoops back in the day)**

above: First day at Churchfields School. I'm on the left and my best friend Rachel is in the middle

below: Big sis duties

left: Marbella. Just wasn't old enough for Ocean Beach yet.

above: Granddad's birthday

right: Me and Granddad

below: Me with Daisy, my 16th
birthday present

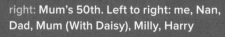

right: Mum's 50th. Left to right: me, Nan,
Dad, Mum (With Daisy), Milly, Harry

above and left: **Arts Ed**

below left: **Meeeee, backstage BGT 2009**

below: **MM and Demi backstage at BGT in costume**

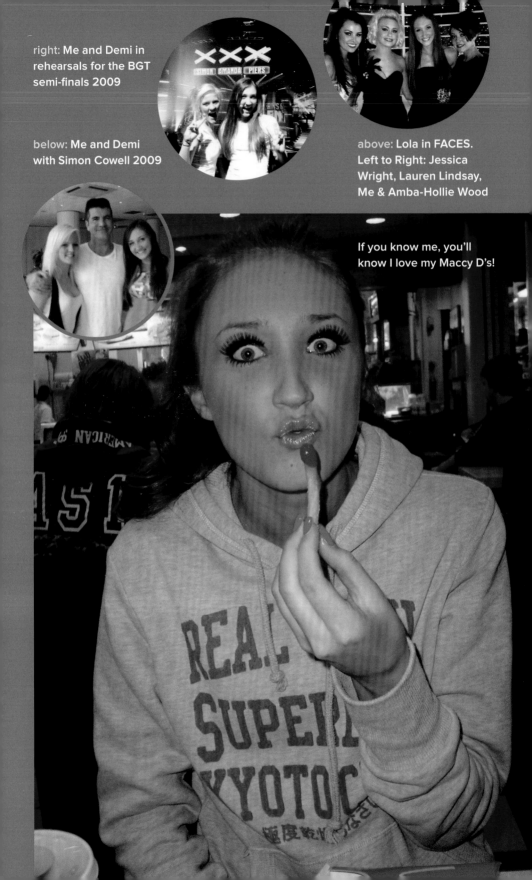

right: Me and Demi in rehearsals for the BGT semi-finals 2009

below: Me and Demi with Simon Cowell 2009

above: Lola in FACES. Left to Right: Jessica Wright, Lauren Lindsay, Me & Amba-Hollie Wood

If you know me, you'll know I love my Maccy D's!

school that everyone fancied. He had the perfect blond bowl cut. At Churchfields, we used to play our own version of TV's *Blind Date*, and, whichever girl won, her prize was always walking around the playground hand in hand with Jason White.

Churchfields' other resident heartthrob was Miles Brett – another boy that everyone fancied, including me. So they were my two earliest crushes, although I didn't go out with either of them, or anyone else for that matter. I was too young and scared. I didn't kiss a boy until much later.

A few years later, I took a shine to a boy at Ravenscourt. All of us girls liked AJ – he was a year older than us, and had that 'bad boy' thing about him. One day, me, AJ and my best friend Emily were all on the train station platform at Leytonstone, and I said I was going to kiss him. How romantic, ha ha. I was so scared, as no one knew I hadn't actually kissed anybody before. Me and AJ walked off to the Leytonstone sign and he leant in to me. I kissed him, and in my head, all I was thinking was, 'Oh my God! What do I do now? When do I put my tongue in?' But I didn't have to worry. He was clearly experienced.

After that, we didn't stop. On the train to school, on the train back, in the hallway at school... AJ was my first kiss, and definitely not my worst.

A year or so later, I was once again with Emily and once again on the train, this time the District Line Tube. I was saying out loud I wanted a boyfriend, so we spent half an hour trying to decide who. It's funny to think how easy it was in them days, picking your boyfriend that quickly!

We threw loads of names in the hat, and one kept coming up. Let's call him Mr First. He was another Ravenscourt boy, but he was a bit different from the others, a bit of a little rude boy, living just round the corner from school and going about on his ped bike. At some point, I decided he was going to be the lucky boy. I can't remember how we got together, but we did. And he became my first real relationship.

I don't know if you really know what love is at the age of sixteen, but I was obsessed with Mr First. Unfortunately that didn't stop him being a bit of a prick to me, the way only a sixteen-year-old boy can be. One of his ex-girlfriends (he was only sixteen, how did he already have ex-girlfriends LOL?) was at a nearby rival stage school. I didn't know her at all, but obviously that didn't stop me hating her. And then, of course, she joined our school. This meant, apparently, that she had to 'pop round to Mr First's' to 'pick up a spare blazer' – because they're always lying about – and I soon heard through the grapevine that she'd got a bit more than a uniform for her troubles. It was right when I was talking to him, I found out. He denied it but it was already clear he was a bit of a playboy. I should have seen the signs.

Whenever I went round to his house to see him, he seemed happy enough to see me, but he didn't want to introduce me to anyone. I seemed to be his big secret. Plus, he didn't make much effort to see me, he always seemed to want to be with his mates instead. Plus, he didn't talk that much to me at school either, come to think of it. At the end of the day, he was a teenager and was probably embarrassed about liking a girl. Boys can be dicks when they fancy someone.

Mr First and I somehow stayed together for about two years in total, and somehow the tables turned between us. He began to show more interest in me, but I started to see him more as a friend.

I was still going out with Mr First when I was about to leave Ravenscourt after three amazing years. This meant I had to audition for different theatre colleges, along with everyone else. I decided to try my luck with Arts Educational School in Chiswick, or ArtsEd as everyone calls it.

This time, my mum applied for all the right grants. She became a pro at knowing exactly what to do. I can't thank my mum enough for what she did back then – putting all her time and effort into making sure she could fund me to go to this new college. She eventually went back to being a florist, where she worked so hard day and night, something she's done ever since, same as my dad. She's worked every day ever since I can remember – they're both amazing.

This college was just down the road from Ravenscourt but miles apart in terms of the kind of people who went there. The list of big names who'd been to ArtsEd was even more impressive – stars like Julie Andrews, Nigel Havers, Darcey Bussell and Will Young. Every musical that goes on in the West End, loads of the people in it come from ArtsEd. When I turned up, buzzing from having passed the audition, people were still seriously posh... apart from me, of course, I was still an Essex girl, but in fact, I didn't actually used to sound like I do now. I'd had elocution lessons at Ravenscourt and in private as part of the training to help us go for all different types of roles, so I didn't sound quite so Essex back then, but I still stood out.

No one else in my year at Ravenscourt moved to ArtsEd, so I was on my own again, and still making that long train journey backwards and forwards from Woodford. Everyone seemed to have loads more money than me – like I said, they were proper posh, but I made some really good friends, and got invited to lots of glamorous parties. Officially, I was still Mr First's girlfriend, but my world was changing very quickly.

One of my friends had a brother called... let's call him Mr Venezuela... and he used to come and collect her from school in his car. I used to spot him from a mile away; me and everyone else – everyone thought he was a sort. Then I went to a party where he turned up and started taking the mickey out of my accent. My comeback to this was always, 'Well, footballers live in Essex,' like that was a really good thing! For some reason I went home on a real high, feeling a bit excited. I realised, not for the first time, that it was probably time that Mr First and I had 'the chat'.

By now, he had become a family friend more than he was my boyfriend, but I knew it was still going to be difficult. One night, I went to Chinawhite in Soho with my gang from college – fake ID as per usual – and Mr Venezuela was there. That night... I know this is terrible, but I kissed him. It was only a kiss, but the guilt I felt inside was a joke.

The next day I arranged to meet Mr First at Holborn Tube station in the centre of town, and he turned up with his bag ready for an overnight stay. Instead, I asked if we could go for a drink, and my heart was pounding. I had a coffee and he had a cloudy apple juice. I remember this day like it was yesterday. I insisted on paying for both drinks, like I thought that would make it all okay. Then I somehow broke it to him that things weren't working any more between us.

Mr First burst into tears in the middle of the café, and said straight away, 'Is it him?' Oh dear! I kept saying, 'It's not him, it's not him,' while inside I was thinking, 'Of course it's him.' The poor boy was really traumatised and eventually I left. It was possibly one of the hardest things I've ever had to do. I loved him but, by now, it was more as a friend, and I think he knew that deep down. I literally sobbed all the way home, then when I got there, my mum started crying. My whole family were actually crying. Everyone liked him. He had become like a family member to us. At the end of the day, we were just both young, and he'll always have that special place in my heart.

A few weeks later, Mr Venezuela took me out on our first proper date. We went off to Wimbledon Village for a meal, and had a really lovely time. What can I tell you? He promised me the world. We went out for a year, and I have to say, it was the most perfect relationship for all of that time. He treated me like a princess, I'd never known anything like it. He lived in Wimbledon, but he went to university in Kingston, and I was so obsessed with him, I got a job in Kingston just to be near him. He and I both got scouted to work at Hollister, and ended up doing all sorts of random shifts. I think we actually only worked a couple of shifts together after all that, and I seemed to spend my life on the train or Tube, going between Woodford, Wimbledon, Kingston and ArtsEd. My life felt complete.

And then, one day, he broke up with me. Yep, just like that. Five little words that don't go anywhere near describing the pain I went through over our relationship coming to an end. We never really argued – I wasn't a shouter back then – but somehow it just stopped working, until one day he sent me a text message saying it was all over. A TEXT MESSAGE – IS HE FUCKING FOR REAL? Finishing it by text... but what can you do? We were both quite young still, and I think he started feeling pressure from family and other people about getting on with his life.

Whatever it was, we went our separate ways, and I was absolutely destroyed when it happened. I called him, he didn't answer. I rang his parents' house, but they wouldn't let me speak to him.

I couldn't deal with seeing him or any of his mates on any social media, so I had to unfollow them all. I had a really good friend at ArtsEd called Imelda, but she was in that group, so I had to unfriend her along with everyone else. They hadn't done anything wrong, but I couldn't handle seeing what they were all up to. I'd left ArtsEd by now, and seeing them live the life I used to lead absolutely killed me. I just never wanted it to end with Mr Venezuela.

I still wanted to talk to Imelda, but I couldn't bring myself to do it. One of my biggest regrets from that time is that Imelda and I lost touch. I'd definitely thank her for being such a good friend to me. But I wasn't seeing anyone. I stopped going out in London. It felt like everything I'd enjoyed had just gone to shit.

Instead, I sat on my bed, sobbing. I didn't know what to do with myself, and I just thought my life was over now Mr Venezuela wasn't in it. At one point, I think I was quite literally hanging on my curtains, crying all these tears, while my friends just stared at me, not knowing what to say. Nobody knew what to do with me. My mum did her best – she gave me all these big lectures about pulling myself together, but I couldn't do it. I was just beside myself. The pain inside me went really deep and nothing took it away. I couldn't eat. I didn't laugh. I don't think I went out for a full six months. That was definitely my first heartbreak, but not the last.

Six months after Mr Venezuela finished with me, just as I was starting to feel a bit better, I received a Facebook message from him, out of the blue, asking me how I was doing.

This is where I want to tell you girls... Don't reply. If he cared, he wouldn't have done it in the first place.

But there I was, brushing my hair, sticking my eyelashes on, ready to have a webcam chat. I didn't even play hard to get. What a twat!

It went really well – we had a nice catch up, and then... nothing. He never contacted me again. So I was broken all over again, except it didn't take me that long to mend this time around.

I got myself a job in a bar, just round the corner from home. I started going out again, and I even started talking to a few boys. For the first time in what seemed like ages, my mind wasn't on Mr Venezuela, thank God.

What really helped to heal my broken heart, though, was the thought of performing again.

During my time at ArtsEd, I worked my arse off, but I wasn't convinced I was the best fit for it. The teachers there were incredibly professional – they had their ways, they just weren't the same as mine. I don't want to sound ungrateful. The training was intense and it definitely made me a better dancer. I reckon if I'd stayed there longer, I would have got a lot better. And they definitely made me a better actor, too. So, don't get me wrong, I did learn a lot of good stuff.

The real problem was the way they taught singing – I just found it all a bit 'by the book'. The teachers were incredibly strict and it turned out they didn't want me to sing the way I naturally sang.

My main course at the college was musical theatre, and that meant two A levels plus other training, but the way I wanted my career to go was never the same way that they wanted. The teachers seemed to want to turn us all into a chorus, like a performing backline, moving and sounding the same, but I was always going to be a little bit different.

Right at the start, they asked us, 'What show do you want to be in when you're older?' and everyone answered with things like *Les Misérables* and *West Side Story*. But I threw a spanner in the works from day one when I said, 'I want my own show, my own world tour.'

One of my mates told me I shouldn't have said that, but I had to tell the truth. I never wanted to be in the chorus; I wanted to be centre stage. I mean, I'd still love to be in a musical, but only if I was the lead.

Then, when we started training, they didn't want me to sing the songs I liked. Instead, it was stuff from old-school musicals, and I just found it all a bit boring. It also knocked my confidence a bit, because that wasn't my natural style – it didn't bring out the best in me, and then I got lots of criticism, so it was all a bit unhelpful really.

I ended up finishing one academic year at ArtsEd, but I didn't go back for the second. It taught me a lot, but, before I left, I was finding it harder and harder to train full-time and still be doing my singing, which is what I really wanted to do. I needed to go for loads of auditions and somehow get my big break. It had even got to the point where I was pulling sickies when I couldn't get the time off to sneak out to an audition.

On one of those afternoons before I left, I was back on the train to my job with Hollister in Kingston, flicking through Twitter, when I spotted a tweet, offering auditions for a girl band. I randomly clicked on it, and it turned out to be for a band called Lola. Apparently, they already had three girls lined up, and were looking for a fourth. Not only that, but the auditions were going to take place in Nu Bar in Loughton, right near my mum's house in Woodford, so it seemed the natural thing to do to sign up and go along. It seems such a long time ago now, when I was a very different person. But that's how I ended up in the wonderful world of *TOWIE*, falling into its dramas for the very first time.

When I got to Nu Bar that day, I had no idea where this could go. The plan was that Lola – which stood for Lovable Outrageous Loud Ambitious – would stand alone as a group, but make cameo appearances on *TOWIE*, the connection being Jess Wright, who was one of the show's big stars and also in the group. When I turned up for the audition, I recognised one of the other girls as Lauren Lindsey, who I used to go with to Saturday school, all them years before. She was sitting in a tracksuit, but she looked really exotic, and it took me a while to realise she had a spray tan. It was the first time I'd ever seen one of those. It wasn't exactly the last though, LOL. (I bet you never thought that, but honestly, I wasn't used to this. My friendship groups weren't from Essex any more. I was spending all my time in London.)

The third girl was Amba-Hollie Wood. The band had been formed a year earlier, but one of their original line-up, Linzi Peel, had left, so they were looking for a newbie.

I had to sing a version of Mariah Carey's 'All I Want for Christmas Is You', and it seemed to go okay. The next day I got a message saying I was through to the next round, which was actually going to be filmed for an episode of *TOWIE*. At this point, I was still licking my wounds about Mr Venezuela, so all I really wanted was to look as nice as possible, in case he saw me on telly. I turned up for the audition at Faces Nightclub in Gants Hill (God, I basically live in there now), and the first person I saw was Mark Wright. He asked me on camera, 'Have you got a boyfriend?' which got me buzzing. In my head I'm thinking, 'Oh my God, him saying that comment, this is going to make Mr Venezuela so jealous.' Mark was the main guy on *TOWIE*, and he made me feel good about myself. I'd just turned eighteen, everyone there was older than me, and I was kind of making it all up as I went along, but one thing I've always had is some balls when it comes to performing. I knew it had gone fine, and they told me there and then I'd got the gig. Literally, the next day, we were in the studio, and life suddenly got really busy.

The four of us girls became really close. We did all sorts of cool things – dressing up for photo shoots, turning up for big events, clubbing together in London. In between all that, we actually recorded an album, met producers, tried out loads of songs and moved between studios, but somehow that side of it never seemed to work. The record companies just thought we were some reality TV joke act, even though we could all actually sing. Jess got a bit more attention because of her *TOWIE* profile already being quite high, but the rest of us were just wandering around hoping to be noticed.

I was never in it for the reality TV side, though. I was soaking everything up, trying to learn about the music industry, finding out how agents and production companies worked. It was all useful stuff, and the best part of all was the friendship between us four girls. In that sense, it was one of the best times of my life, and it was what did the trick in getting me over the heartbreak of Mr Venezuela when everything else had failed. Being in Lola gave me a focus, a reason to get up in the morning. I'd say to any young girl going through a similar thing:

> Don't fall apart like I did. Don't panic like I did. Make a plan, get busy, and, if you can, have a laugh about it with your mates. Be open, because everyone's gone through it. And always, always talk to your mum.

By the time I was having fun with my Lola girls, I'd completely forgiven Mr Venezuela for all that pain. Unlike some I could mention, he never gave me a reason to hate him, and we're still friends to this day. It was clear at the time that I didn't really fit into in his future, and it soon became clear that he would have had trouble fitting into mine. I was in a bubble with him back then, always trekking over to West London to see him or to work or something, and our split forced me back to my roots in the east of the city.

Growing up, I'd always associated this area with bullying and illness, and it seemed like I had most of my fun away from it. But for the first time, I got to know my own area properly. Now all my friends are here as well as my family, it's a different world for me – it makes me really happy, and I can truthfully say I'm an Essex girl at heart.

My top tips for getting over an ex

💋 Fly to Marbella for a season (but don't quit the season after only a month — you'll understand why later in this book)

💋 Be with your girls (but don't get drunk and cause a row with them all)

💋 Treat yourself with LV bags (but don't go too crazy, or you'll end up crying even more)

💋 Get a good blow-dry, a tan and some eyelashes and get down to Faces (don't sit at home and hang off your curtains)

💋 Get yourself a dog. They will always love you whatever #DaisyCuddles

💋 I've said it before, but I'll say it again. Talk to your mates. Before you know it, you'll be laughing again

💋 And always, always, talk to your mum

I have loads of amazing memories of that year of Lola
– partying, nights out at Movida, glasses of Cristal, VIP
invitations, and properly getting over Mr Venezuela. I
opened myself up to a whole brand new world – the
Essex life. This was me changing and I loved it – hanging
out with older people, getting my confidence back and
generally finding myself.

But, Lola started to run a bit dry, and I'd run out of
ideas about how to promote myself. However much I
wanted to delay being in the real world, it was time to get
grown up and sort out my bank balance because I was
skint. I was driving around in a shitty old car and I couldn't
even afford to put £5 of petrol in it. It was time to face
reality: I needed a job.

My mate Lauren was also in Lola, and she used to work at Nu Bar in Loughton, so she said she might be able to get me a job. It's shut down now, but, back then when we were talking about it, Nu Bar was THE place to go. The owner was a guy called Adam – he knew everyone in the area. All the girls who worked there were considered proper sorts. It was in the best position on Loughton High Road, and every Friday, Saturday and Sunday it wasn't just busy, it was packed. Adam had somehow got the mix just right – football on the screens, and later, DJs coming out to play. Loads of my mates ended up there anyway at weekends, so getting a job there seemed like a no-brainer.

Lauren took me to meet Adam's mum, who helped manage the place, and she asked me straight away, 'Do you want a shift? Are you free Saturday?' I thought, 'Shit, this is it.' So I turned up on time, got through all the jobs I was given, and more importantly for me, got loads of attention from the boys there. I'd never had that before, through all my years of theatre school, and I thought, 'Wow, I like this.'

I got more and more shifts at Nu Bar, and, when I wasn't working, I'd end up going in there anyway, as I got to know so many people. It became my new world.

I'd been there a few months when I started talking to a cute pot boy. Let's call him Mr Pinocchio – that's short for

Pinocchio, as he did like to tell a few porkie pies. The good news is, he became my official rebound and helped get me over Mr Venezuela. The bad news is, he was a little shit. And little, literally, as it turned out. I was eighteen by then, and Mr Pinocchio told me he was too. He'd actually just turned seventeen, but that was just one of his many porkies to me. He used to phone me and say he was calling from work, when actually he was still in sixth-form college. He told me the reason he didn't have a car was because he'd written it off. He had a vivid imagination, I'll give him that.

One day, about six months into our relationship, I was lying on his bed, and I spotted a school picture with the caption 'Leavers' Year' but the dates were all wrong. I looked around his room more carefully, and there seemed to be suits lying around. But then I opened the door to his wardrobe, and all I could see were school books. I was fuming and also confused! I called him upstairs and asked him about the picture. He immediately started telling me a really detailed story about how his parents had pulled him out of school, MOVED TO SPAIN and then come back, so he'd gone down a school year. You have to credit the boy, he really could think on his feet.

We went out then to walk his dogs, and, out of the blue, he asked me, 'If I was younger than you, would you still go out with me?' He later admitted it. Also, my brother's girlfriend Jordan had been at his school, so the truth soon came out.

We stayed together for another six months or so, but it was never going to work. I used to write him long lists, trying to make him change – a bit more of this, a bit less of that... basically trying to turn him into Mr Venezuela. Well, that was never going to work. So, sooner or later, another relationship went to shit.

After Mr Pinocchio and I broke up, I went into work and was chatting to a boy called Tom Pearce. He'd just joined the cast of *TOWIE*, and we knew loads of the same people. Just as Tom was taking my number, Mr Pinocchio appeared in front of us, saying, 'You know we're going out.' Tom said, 'Really? I'm not interested if you've got a boyfriend.' He walked off and I ended up having a row with Mr P. 'You're ruining it for me,' I shouted at him, and that was the end of things between us.

God, these stories sound so petty now, but at the time they seemed like a big deal. When I think back about that time, Mr Pinocchio was just too young and didn't mean no harm. He's a sweet boy, really.

No more broken hearts for me, I decided after that, and I would say it was at that point I officially became a party girl. I loved going to work in that place, chatting to all the customers, getting great tips, knowing everyone. The blokes who came in were terrible, cocky Essex boys, but we had such a laugh. If I wasn't on shift, I was in there, still chatting, doing shots, throwing up in the loos. I loved every minute.

Tom and I went out a few times after that, but he messed me about a bit, he wasn't in the mood for settling down. In the meantime, Lauren had a new boyfriend who had a big group of friends, and I soon got drawn into it. For the first time in my life, I was a member of the cool gang. The girls were nice, the boys were smooth and cocky, and then I came across the smoothest, cockiest one of them all.

10

What can I tell you about this time in my life? Well, I guess everyone's got a moment where it all seems to go a bit pear-shaped for one reason or another. For me, it was the two years that followed me bumping into this one boy. Looking back, I think of this whole time now as the dip in my life, so that's what we'll call him, The Dip.

He was from Essex. He was two years older than me and he was one of them cheeky, cocky boys from the area.

He walked into Nu Bar and we were introduced. He'd just got a brand new car, a big 4X4, and the other boys were all taking the mickey. He was being all flirty and that to me, and then he offered to drop me off in his brand new shiny car. If the worst mistake I ever made was meeting this boy, then probably the worst decision I ever made was accepting that lift home.

A few days later, he took me on a date to... Virgin Active, as you do. We couldn't get in the pool area, so we ended up playing crazy golf instead. I thought, 'This kid's mad,' but I loved it – he was just different from anyone else I'd come across. We clicked pretty instantly and that was it. I don't know why it all happened so quickly, but by the time we'd been on a few more dates, I was completely in love with him. Looking back, I'm really not sure why – he was a little prick most days, but it didn't stop me.

It was a really confusing time. We'd have a great time together, hanging out by ourselves, but then he'd go out with the boys and be a massive flirt. When I was working shifts at Nu Bar, people would come in and start telling me he was being flirty around loads of girls.

Whenever I went back to him with it, I should have listened more carefully when he told me, 'I don't want a girlfriend. You and I are SEEING each other.' He kept telling me, but I didn't want to hear it. I should have seen the signs, but I was just so happy to be hanging out with him. I can remember lying in his room, cuddling up to him, then turning over and silently crying because of that nervous feeling in my stomach, not knowing if he was actually mine, hoping he was but scared I was kidding myself.

One night, I walked into the bar to start my shift, and a boy came straight over to me and asked if I was still seeing The Dip. When I said yes, he showed me a text message he'd got from some blondie on holiday. In her text, she'd written to him, 'Someone just said [The Dip] is with a girl with brown hair in Nu Bar. What's going on?'

I thought, 'Hang on. I'M the girl with the brown hair, but who the hell is this blondie?!'

I rang The Dip straight away and asked him, 'Who is she?' Well, apparently, it was some girl he used to see who he was having trouble getting rid of. Bollocks. The truth was, he was still sleeping with her. I was so stupid. If I was seeing him about twice a week, she clearly was too.

As a result of that disaster, did I immediately dump him? Did I listen to my mates and my mum, and never speak to him again? Er, no. Instead, we became official. For fuck's sake.

I do think he loved me in his own special way and knew I was a bit more important to him than he realised, but the boy just couldn't help himself. We decided to give it a go, but the experience changed me a lot as a person. When anyone goes on about my temper, my mum always says that I was completely 'normal' (whatever that is), polite and well-behaved until I started meeting boys, or should I say, started coming up against boys who promised me one thing and then went behind my back and did the opposite. I do believe it's enough to drive any girl a bit mad being treated like that, and then the girls get a really bad rep for not being able to handle that kind of treatment. Why SHOULD they be able to handle it? What about the boys who dish it out? Anyway... I agree with my mum, and I would say the change in me happened once I made that shit decision to 'become official' with The Dip.

We'd decided to give it a proper go, but I became constantly paranoid about where he was and who he was with. Someone told me once, 'He's got his arm around a blonde girl,' and I phoned him to check. Next thing I knew, he came flying into the bar, he had a fight and he told me it was a lie, all of which convinced me it couldn't possibly be true. Er... I don't think he was shagging other girls, but I just never felt like I was that one special girl for him. It was a shame, because it knocked all the confidence out of me, which I'd finally got back after what I'd gone through with Mr Venezuela. He always seemed to ask questions like, 'What were you up to last night?' – which I realise now was a sign of his own doubts. One evening, we walked into the bar together and he pecked a girl on the lips, but if I even smiled at some other bloke, he could get nasty. He left me in tears so many times.

My mum didn't like him at all, as she could see what my relationship with him was doing to me. Sometimes, he'd surprise her and be really nice, but overall, there were just too many dramas surrounding him. I was moody with my family, or I'd get sent home from work. I wasn't doing myself any favours there – I was rowing with other girls, shouting at them from across the bar, always blaming the girl, never him. Why do we do that?

Nu Bar wasn't going so well for me by now, bearing in mind I was always either crying, shouting or being sent home. The Dip had broken up with me by now, but don't get me wrong, I was still running around there and sleeping with him. Then one night, a few girls came into the bar and walked straight up to me. One said, 'Look, Megan, we were at a house party of The Dip's the other week, and he didn't do anything, you have nothing to worry about. I feel for you, I've been heartbroken myself.' She even took me outside for a heart to heart and I told her everything that was going wrong between us. Well, guess what? It turned out she was banging him. In fact, turns out she'd banged him and her best pal had given him a blow job.

Another evening, I got into another fight with two other girls. I remember having my hair pulled, and Lauren managing to pull me away from them. She was shouting at me, 'Look at yourself, look what he's done to you.'

I was a mess. I have no idea why he had such a hold over me – I couldn't even tell you anything that was so special. All I can say is that he was everything to me. He made me laugh, he could be quite caring when we were on our own, but that was it.

Things came to a head one night. As usual, we were in Nu Bar, and, as usual, The Dip and I were giving each

other a hard time. I thought he said something horrible
in my direction, so I threw everything within reach at him
across the bar – yeah, that's right, every single drink I
could see I dashed at him – until the bouncers came and
picked me up to get me out of there. You know things
have turned pretty bad when bouncers who are employed
to get rid of the messiest customers have to actually throw
out one of the bar staff. How embarrassing.

On my way out, two girls walked in, and – I'll never
be sure why they did this to me, considering I was quite
clearly already broken – one of the girls punched me in
the face. Don't ask me why, but her mate joined in – she
pulled my hair from the back of me and I ended up on
the floor. The bouncers picked me back up, but I was
screaming. By now the lights had gone on throughout the
bar, the music had stopped and everyone was staring. The
bouncers were doing their best to hold me down, trying to
calm me, but I was a lunatic. I lied and told them I was fine
so they would let me go. Then, I ran out onto the street
and screamed, 'Where are they?'

I was running around the streets of Loughton on
my own, with my friends coming after me. The Dip had
disappeared by now, he clearly didn't care what happened
to me, but I was also past caring about myself, by the
looks of things. I was in such a rage, I didn't realise I'd
accidentally bumped into the wrong group of people
outside somewhere. It turned into a huge fight – some of

The Dip's friends tried to help me, but I got pulled to the floor. I remember my face hitting the kerb – my nose was grazed and my hands covered in grit. The police arrived, sat me down on the steps and just looked at me while I sat shouting at them. They threatened to put me in a cell for the night if I didn't pipe down. By now, it was three o'clock in the morning and I was very, very low.

I woke up in my own bed at home with a sore head and a very bruised heart. I wanted to watch the CCTV from the bar, to try to understand how it had all got so far out of hand. I saw myself arguing with The Dip, drinking and being so out of control, but the worst part of the footage was when he just walked away, while I was standing in the bar screaming. I had been so affected by someone who just didn't care, and it made me really sad. As for the fight, well the footage confirmed what I already knew. At least that hadn't been my fault, so I reported it to the police, but eventually I let it go.

Me and him and our toxic relationship didn't just go wrong in Essex either. Towards the end of it all, I decided to move to Marbella with a friend to get away from everything. I got a job at Tibu Nightclub right by the beach and it all seemed to be going okay, but guess who turned up on a boys' holiday? Mr Dip himself. I was walking along the strip in a yellow bikini and wedges when I spotted him. I couldn't believe it, but I walked over and he just said, 'All right, Meg?' like we were back in Nu Bar.

All pretty predictable. We both got drunk, had a huge row that got me sacked from Tibu, screamed at each other, slept with each other and promised to get back together – PROPERLY this time.

I was in Marbella for a month – I was meant to stay for the whole season, but the next morning I rang my mum and told her I was coming home early. There were auditions for *The X Factor* brewing at this point, but that wasn't the real reason. Deep down, I wanted to come back to be with The Dip again.

Before I flew home, I went to his hotel, and a girl – the same girl who'd slept with him, and then pretended to be my friend – was in the foyer. I thought I recognised her but I wasn't sure. As I was walking up to her, I thought she looked a bit strange, a bit... white, and as I got up close, I realised it was because she was covered in fire extinguisher foam. She swore at me, just as she was being thrown out by the hotel bouncers. I carried on up to his room, but when I got to his floor, I could see the whole corridor was covered in fire extinguisher foam, the same white foam I'd just seen all over the girl. I walked along the corridor, thinking, 'Please don't let it be his room, please don't let it be his.' But of course it was. There he was, naked in his room, with fire extinguisher foam all over him. And what did I do? Did I walk away? No, I slept with him.

Looking back, I think The Dip treating me so badly turned me into a bit of a psycho, which probably made him even more distant. One time when I was staying with him, I went through his phone and I found a message from another girl saying, 'Are you coming to see me this weekend?' I woke him up, and he said he never went to meet her, but I ended up getting the girl's number and calling her up. She said he didn't come to meet her. Okay, he never went through with these actions, but fuck me, why do this in the first place? He clearly couldn't help himself. I had to phone my mum and ask her to come and get me. On the way home in the car, she was fuming and she said, 'You're never seeing that boy again, look what he's turned you into.'

She was right. I needed help. I was doing anything I could think of just to get his attention. It wasn't normal behaviour. I was turning up at his house at four o'clock in the morning – paying a cabbie to drive me all the way from mine to his, turning up at his parents' house, knocking on his door and shouting, 'Please can you let me in?' At first, he'd say, 'Fuck off, Meg, you psycho,' but eventually he'd let me in. Then we'd sleep together, even though I knew he didn't really want to be with me. He wanted to be single, he'd told me that, and it was a terrible feeling, having sex with someone, loving them so much, but knowing that feeling's not coming back at you. I wanted everything with him, and he didn't want any of it, but I just didn't care. I was obsessed.

> In case anyone reading this sorry tale hasn't got the message loud and clear by now, I want to spell it out to any girls who might be going through something similar in their own lives: get out now. Find someone who treats you better.

You need to get out now before you get in even more trouble and your self-esteem sinks even lower than you thought possible. Trust me, there is no worse feeling than crying on your own, coming home drunk, throwing up and being picked up by your parents because you can't look after yourself, all because you've been brought so low by heartbreak.

It scares me now, the thought of how I behaved, how badly I treated my body as well as my head. Maybe on some level I thought that if I suffered enough and I was dramatic enough, The Dip would eventually come running. But now I realise the world doesn't work like that.

Our relationship lasted two-and-a-half years in total. It was far too long a time for something that took over my life.

Finally, I went to his house one night after yet another argument. As usual, all I wanted was for him to love me like I loved him, but on this occasion, the argument got so bad that eventually his mum came upstairs because of all the screaming. She told us to stop – she said, 'You're not right together.'

The tipping point came when I was sacked from Nu Bar because of that night, for throwing the drinks, and also calling the head bouncer a fat c**t. So that was that. I was asked to leave. A few weeks later, I begged for my job back, and the new owners agreed to let me come back on the condition that I tidied up my act, and apologised to the bouncer.

It was time to get my shit together.

11

Two weeks later, I was sitting at my desk in my office...
I know, I know, Megan McKenna did actually have a
real job, back in the day. Who'd have thought it?
But once I made the decision that things needed to
change, I went and got myself a job at an estate agent's
in Loughton, and I enjoyed it more than I thought
I would.

I tried to put my past with The Dip behind me. The
new me involved drinking less, shouting less, crying less
and making new friends where I could find them. One of
these was a girl called Connie. She told me she wasn't
over her ex-boyfriend either, so I told her all about mine
and we cried on each other's shoulders. We really clicked,
and promised to look after each other.

A few weeks later... sorry, everyone... me and The Dip got back together in some small fashion. He was about to a buy a nightclub in Essex, and we soon fell into the same messed-up routine. I told him I'd become mates with Connie, and the first thing he said was, 'She's a slag, that girl.' I thought that was a bit strange; I didn't even know their paths had crossed. Anyway, I ignored him and stayed friends with her – all part of the new independent me.

Well, that didn't exactly last long. Me and The Dip had ended again, and one night, Connie and I were sitting in my kitchen. We were having a cup of tea after we'd been to Westfields shopping centre, and she suddenly burst into tears. She said that she had to tell me something.

'I slept with The Dip.'

I was in shock. We went through the dates on my phone, and it turned out it was the first Christmas after we'd started seeing each other that this had happened. Back then, it was before we were official, but come on, we were sleeping together and we'd given each other Christmas presents.

Once again, The Dip made me lose my shit. As for her, I was almost speechless that night. She didn't owe me anything back in the day when she slept with him, but... why make friends with me, watching me cry over him, hearing all my stories, pretending to look after me, pretending she didn't even know him when she'd been there herself?

I told her to leave that night and told her I didn't want to speak to her ever again. After that, she turned up at Nu Bar pretty regularly, but we never got it sorted. We had lots of rows, and it was all pretty dramatic. I was more angry with her than I was with him by then.

Because Connie had become a really good friend to me, I'd asked her to come up to London with me for a thing a few weeks before. She'd happily tagged along, which meant it was Connie standing next to me when I went for my very first audition for a new MTV dating show.

To be honest, I didn't really know what the show was about, as there wasn't much buzz when I applied to go on it. All I'd heard was, it was a new show in a faraway place, and they were looking for cool people to find love on an island. This sounded perfect for me!

For my very first meeting with the producers, I turned up at Cirque le Soir nightclub in Soho, all glammed up, Connie by my side. Even that first meeting didn't go smoothly. When I turned up and asked for the MTV table, I was told, 'Sorry, no MTV here tonight.' I was gutted, even when the rep texted me to say they were in another club but on their way, and they'd be with me soon. I thought, 'You're mugging me off.' I thought it was a load of shit and got drunk at the bar.

By the time they actually arrived, I was completely smashed, having the time of my life, when someone tapped me on the shoulder and said, 'We're from MTV.' I was standing there, paralytic, and I couldn't believe this was actually real. I think me being in that state might actually have helped me, because I didn't really care what I said. They took lots of photos, and that was it. They said they'd be in touch.

I was invited for a further audition, but – not exactly great timing – it turned out to be the day after Connie dropped her bombshell on me. So when I went to see them again, my eyes were still puffy from crying, my nose was still running, I was basically still hysterical. Before this meeting, I went into the bar next door and downed a Jägerbomb. That probably didn't help.

> Here's a quick tip from me to you girls: Don't back Jägers when you're emotionally fucked. It makes things even more fucked.

At this point, I still thought I was going on a dating show to meet new single guys and get away from my shit life. They even said that to me, but before the auditions started, they wanted me to tell them the lowdown on my relationships to get an insight into who I was, what kind of guys I went for, and who I would avoid.

I told them I really couldn't talk about my most recent ex, I was still too upset about him and the whole situation, but they were really kind to me, sat me down, got me a cup of tea and asked me loads of questions all about the sorry state of my love life. Sophie and Jake were the casting producers (I still talk to them now.) They asked me about my past relationships and about my mates. I told them everything, up to and including the situation with Connie, and it felt good to get it all off my chest. I really opened up to them, even saying at one point, 'You might not understand, but I really need to get out of Essex for a while.' They could tell I was genuinely hurt and I'm sure that's what got me the show.

I actually thought I was going on a show called *Are You the One?* I thought it would be a chance to escape my problems for a bit, go somewhere glamorous and get some sun, plus I thought it might lead to something else bigger and better. I was after new experiences, new faces, anything to get me away from The Dip.

But fuck me, this couldn't haven't been anything further from that. I was entering... *Ex on the Beach.* The whole point of THIS show is to pitch together eight single girls and boys looking for love on a summer holiday in paradise. Sounds good, right?

The only spanner in the works is that these eight singletons get joined by their ex-partners. Couldn't have been worse for me, really.

The producers probably hoped they could get The Dip himself to appear on the show at some point, and I know they asked him. As it happened, none of my exes agreed to do it, so instead I rocked up on my own. But even without an ex in sight, after my tearful, drunken rant when I first spoke to them, they must have realised I brought more than my share of drama with me. Perfect casting! Or at least, that's what I thought they were after. I didn't realise at that point that, when it came to me, they had an extra little secret card up their sleeve.

12

One of the reasons I didn't think it could be *Ex on the Beach* was because, that show normally takes place in Marbella. THIS show was going to be somewhere far away and tropical. I didn't know where, but all I got told was to pack my bag for a month and to bring my passport. By the time I got to the airport, I still had no idea where I was travelling, but the chaperone slipped up and said something like, 'I've got my British phone, but I've also got my Mexican phone.' Ha ha! At that point, I had to hand over my own phone, but I quickly messaged my mum to say, 'I think I'm going to Mexico.' I also had my iPod in my bag somewhere, and that had WiFi on it. When we stopped over in New York for our connecting flight, I quickly sent my mate a message on Facebook, to tell my mum where I was and that I was safe.

We finally got to Cancún and I was allowed to make a phone call home, as long as I didn't reveal where I was. So we had this pantomime of me dialling home and saying, 'I've arrived somewhere safely, but I can't tell you where.' My mum obviously knew already by then, but she went along with it.

When we got to the hotel, we had to be kept in hiding for a good few days. This was so me and the rest of the cast didn't bump into each other. All the secrecy meant I had to stay in the apartment – no swimming pool, but a massive telly, so that was something. I kept begging the chaperone to tell me which show it was, but she wouldn't say a word. After a few days, she didn't have to. On that same massive telly, I was watching *Ex on the Beach*, and the opening credits were very similar to the VTs I'd filmed back home when I'd been packing my bags. It dawned on me, 'Shit, could this be *Ex on the Beach*?' These scenes looked too similar to what I'd just filmed back in Essex.

Finally, I got to the beach where I was about to go on and make my debut on this new dating show. I was allowed to have as many drinks as I wanted, so I backed tequila and Jägerbombs. Then the producers walked me round to the beach front – they said to me, 'Do you know what show you're on yet?' and I said, 'I have a feeling, but I'm not sure.' They said, 'Walk on, you'll be filmed from this moment onwards,' and as I walked round, it was the familiar *Ex on the Beach* bar.

I walked up, got given a coconut, and, as I stood there, I thought, 'I'm fucked.'

One of the lads was Kirk Norcross off *TOWIE*, and he was really cute, but it was a bloke called Bear who initially caught my eye. He was really good-looking and we had banter, but from the very first night he was playing me off against a girl called Amy. I mean, come on, I'd left Nu Bar to get away from all of this, but now it was happening all over again – the only difference was, I was in a bloody bikini in front of a TV crew.

Then, a couple of nights after we arrived, I found myself in a strange situation at the dining-room table – I was arguing with Bear and I felt my temper boil up. For some reason, Bear accused me of liking Kirk for his money, and I just saw red. I ended up shouting and walking off, which seemed a bit dramatic even to me. I couldn't give two shits about Bear, so why was I screaming at him? Clearly, running away from Essex wasn't the right choice. I just brought all my baggage with me, and was taking out my hurt over The Dip on Bear.

Then Amy's ex-boyfriend Jordan turned up, and he made things even more complicated.

During our intro videos, I'd been asked to describe my ideal man. I'd said things like 'tall, tanned and cheeky'. Well, Jordan turned up, and, guess what? He was tall, tanned, very cheeky. He was from Cardiff, and he'd already been on another show called *The Magaluf*

Weekender so he wasn't nervous at all. In his introduction video, he went on about being 'ready for something serious', but in the villa he made it clear he wanted to party. He was a proper laugh and we just clicked.

Things got a bit more complicated when Bear kept trying it on with me. As I said, he was very good-looking, but pretty soon I made up my mind to stick with Jordan, and I still think I made the right choice.

By now, the producers had realised they could make really easy telly out of me – they just had to feed me with tequila and then watch me explode. My temper was getting worse and worse in that villa. I kept shouting at people, and THEN Jordan's ex-girlfriend turned up.

She was really pretty with big fake tits – she'd clearly been sent in to stir up trouble between me and Jordan, and it worked. They immediately went off on a date, leaving me to sulk in the villa. When they got back, they seemed really close. He was definitely enjoying playing me off against her – probably because I'd been getting lots of attention up until that point and suddenly it was his turn, which is reasonable – so I kicked off again, right on cue. The producers did love to rile us all up. They used to say to me, 'Go on, stir it up tonight, do your worst,' so I would. I used to think, 'Sod it, what do I care?' Part of me was thinking, 'I'm never going to see these people again,' while the other part of me was getting genuinely drawn into the drama of it all. Plus, free Jägerbombs on tap didn't exactly help matters. Really and truly, underneath all this anger was just a broken girl.

Despite that little bit of romantic drama, it wasn't actually the boys who really set me off in the villa. It was a few of the girls, speaking about me behind my back. I felt like I'd done everything I could to make friends with them – lending them clothes, talking about stuff – and it had seemed all right at first. The way they behaved towards me took me all the way back to Woodbridge – it made me really paranoid and I just didn't know how to deal with it.

After years of having a bunch of really good female friends, it brought everything back from a time when it was the opposite – all them memories of being picked on in the school corridor, and it made me lose it in the villa. I could go from nought to ten in seconds, over something really basic like food. Anyone watching the show must have thought I was off my nut to start with, but for me it was about not being respected all over again.

By now I was getting a reputation as an unpredictable psycho, based on a number of incidents that looked like I was kicking off for no reason. Well, let me tell you how one of those incidents really went down.

The producers sent most of the girls off on a salon day, basically so they could start bitching about me. The other Megan – 'Welsh Megan' – had been pretty quiet, but she got it in her head that I was getting above myself. She was saying that I thought it had become 'the Megan show', and that I needed to calm down. It was probably just her way of getting some airtime, but it did the job. Some other girls joined in, and everyone else seemed to be rising to it, instead of rising above it.

Later, at the dinner table, Bear stirred things up as usual between Welsh Megan and me, telling me they'd all been talking about me. Then she appeared beside me, telling me we had to go for a chat. She even picked up my plate like she was my schoolteacher. After being bitched about all day, and then them ganging up on me at the dinner table, I wasn't having any of it.

'No, no. Everyone. Fucking no,' I said. 'I don't want to talk right now.'

I walked off, leaving them to more bitching, but I suddenly realised I'd left my dinner behind, and I was actually quite hungry, so I went back in.

What I didn't realise until I came back was that the girls had thought it would be funny to eat my food. Now everybody in that villa knew about my food allergies, that I was on a special diet because I couldn't eat any wheat or gluten. But instead of looking after me, one girl stole my food, which was ham and cheese that night. This girl – the same one who insisted on having chicken every morning for her diet, plus, if I'm honest, was struggling herself for airtime by now – took it upon herself to shovel a load of ham and cheese in her mouth at the table and start prancing around, mimicking me. I couldn't believe it when

I saw what was happening. Why would you do that when someone has an actual illness, and they physically can't eat anything else? She was thirty years old, for goodness' sake – she was meant to be the mature one in that villa. I tried explaining it to her and everyone else, that I couldn't eat anything else on the table because of my allergies. I was feeling really isolated by now, but everyone just thought it was a joke.

It was like being at Woodbridge all over again, and I just couldn't handle it. I couldn't believe her behaviour, and I got to that point again where I couldn't control my temper. I kicked off majorly and started shouting the place down. I called this girl a c**t, and the next thing I knew, we were face to face, threatening to beat each other up. Jordan had to get me out of the room, and I heard Vicky Pattison shouting, 'Someone get the bird some fucking Dairylea,' which would've been actually quite funny if I'd been in the mood for it. But this wasn't the time.

People thought that it happened because I just get hangry. Don't get me wrong, I do. But on that occasion, they were taking the mickey out of something really serious and that just felt unfair.

13

Straight after all that trouble with the girls, I got myself in more trouble with the boys. Those producers really knew what they were doing, ha ha. Next thing I knew, they'd sent another ex into the house called Rogan, aka the world's biggest flirt. I got into loads of trouble with Jordan, because Rogan and I had to touch lips during some crappy tequila game. Jordan started mugging me off, so I accepted Rogan's invitation to the penthouse suite and it caused a massive stir. But all we did was drink champagne, and I ended up leaving. I just wanted to get back at Jordan because he'd messed me about with his ex.

Things were a bit tense between me and Jordan. Everyone was playing a game of truth or dare, which led to me having to kiss Rogan. Five minutes later, Jordan was getting me back twice as hard with the other girls during a game of spin the bottle – I was sitting there fuming. The next thing I knew, it was all over between us, and I was sitting in my room crying.

Looking back, I've no idea why. I didn't love Jordan, not properly, I just got sucked into the drama of it all. At this point, I'd had so many tantrums and breakdowns over tiny things that even one of the producers, Jake, was telling me to pull myself together. He definitely had a point, but the timing couldn't have been worse for another ex to turn up.

Jordan – being all Billy Big Balls about being single again – went off to the beach with Rogan and Bear, waiting for some girl to turn up, while the rest of us waited back at the villa. When Rogan and Bear came back in with no Jordan, my heart sank. Then they said who he was with, and my heart went through the floor. Remember I told you them producers had a secret card up their sleeves when it came to me? Of course they did. It turned out Jordan was on yet another date. With one of Bear's exes. Who happened to be a girl from Essex – and guess what? It was Connie. What the actual fuck?

As far as I was concerned, this was worse than even The Dip turning up. This wasn't just an ex, this was an ex-friend who had shagged my ex. And now Jordan was out on a date with her. Fuck my life.

We were all told we were going to a nightclub, so I got glammed up and was ready to enjoy myself with everyone else. But when we got there, they held everyone back and told me I had to go in first. They told me, 'Megan, go up to the bar and order a round of Jägerbombs.' As I walked in, I looked to the left, and there was a massive candlelit dinner laid out by the pool. And guess who were sitting there hand in hand? Jordan and Connie. I was then told that they'd already had a kiss. I tried to keep it together, and I walked across and stood with the other girls. To everyone else, we looked like the cast of *Mean Girls*, and I was Regina George, but what people didn't realise was that this just brought back all the hurt from my days with The Dip.

I genuinely thought I was hallucinating when I saw her. The look on my face, the smile on hers, the panic on Jordan's, the shock on the other girls' – it was all too much. I'm sure it was amazing TV, but inside, well, I was already cut up to shit by this stage of the show, and then this happened. To see her sitting there... One of the other girls asked me, 'Are you all right?' I didn't know what to do – it was clear everyone wanted me to have a confrontation with her. At this point in my life, I had no respect for myself and had nothing to lose any more. I thought, 'Fuck it, I'm going to talk to her.'

Connie walked over with one of the girls who didn't like me – who was loving every minute of all this, obviously, building up her own part – and I just said, 'Why are you even here?'

She started to speak, but I was just warming up, telling her, 'I don't give a fuck about your opinions.' Then I happened to notice that her hair was looking a bit frizzy, so I added, 'Do you want to get some straighteners on your hair because you look like a fucking lion.'

I find some of these lines a bit embarrassing now if I'm honest. I was just saying stupid things because I was drunk, but all my one-liners kept coming out, including the one where I said, 'Babe, you look like a mop.'

Then we had a proper row about The Dip – that was always going to happen. It was getting really heated, and the producers were whispering to me, 'Push her in the pool,' but I couldn't. I'd probably have been chucked in as well. They were probably saying the same thing to her. Like I said, they do like to rile it up. I managed to drag myself away, but I was beside myself. I was genuinely livid that I had to face her again. Afterwards, I was being interviewed about it, and, even with all my attitude on the outside and the Jägerbombs on the inside, it was clear I was still cut up, saying, 'Why do you think I'm here? I'm trying to get over the shit I've had in the past.' I know people look at me like I'm a psycho, but I'm hurting, and this pain was 100 per cent genuine.

The next day, which was going to be the grand finale of the series, Connie and I actually had a heart to heart in the villa. This time I was sober, and it felt good talking to her. I decided to forgive her, and I think that was probably my first real step in getting over the whole drama with The Dip.

During that final day, Jordan and I also had a heart to heart and became boyfriend and girlfriend. I ended up bringing him back home with me. My poor family! Only a month before, they'd seen me off to the airport, upset and heartbroken over The Dip still. The next thing they know, here I am returning with some Welsh kid and announcing, 'It's only going to work if Jordan moves to Essex. Is it okay if he moves in with us?'

My parents had had a tiny bit of warning. I'd phoned my mum from Mexico and told her I had a boyfriend. She said, 'Okay, but you haven't done anything, have you?' I knew exactly what she meant. The last thing she'd said to me before I walked out that door in England three weeks before was, 'Enjoy yourself, just don't have sex on TV.' Shit!

So I knew what was coming, but at the time, I swerved it and said, 'No, of course not.' Then I got home and realised I had to come clean before the show aired. She wasn't cool about it, but she dealt with it, and my mum has too big a heart to hold a grudge. But I have to say it's my biggest regret, especially when I watched the show back and saw that they'd sped it up, played 'Don't Stop Me Now' by Queen and shown Jordan whacking his head on top of the bunkbed. What a prat! Also, I was gutted to see

Jordan bragging about it. 'I've put more groundwork in than Alan fucking Titchmarsh,' he said on camera. I mean, it's a good line, but like I said, I regret it massively, and it's something I'm not proud of.

What was I thinking?! My family were nice enough to let Jordan live with us for six months. I guess at that point in my life, they just thought, well, whatever happens and whoever he is, he couldn't possibly cause as many problems as old Dippy.

'Never had a real job'? Check out my CV:

Scott's Hairdressers

Reason for leaving: They made me clean a toilet

My Dad's Print Business

Reason for leaving: I had to pack boxes with cab cards in the freezing cold. It would take me eight hours uninterrupted until it was finished!

The Doors at Warehouse and 195

Reason for leaving: I only lasted a few weeks

Catch Fish Restaurant

Reason for leaving: Cleaning glasses wasn't for me. I lasted a day, didn't even collect my wages

My Mum's Flower Shop

Reason for leaving: Firstly, I should explain it's joined to the undertaker's where they hold the dead bodies. I couldn't deal with helping to decorate the coffins, or being next door to the chapel generally. It's not for the faint-hearted!

Switch and Nu Bar bar work

Reason for leaving Switch: Boring

Reason for leaving Nu Bar: Err... See chapters 9 and 10. It's complicated LOL

Strawberry Glow Sunbed Shop

Reason for leaving: No reason! I loved this job, worked there for years. My boss Mike is a legend and we're still very good friends now

Estate Agents

Reason for leaving: *Ex on the Beach* (this was my only full-time job, and it was shit!)

14

Between filming that first series of *Ex on the Beach* and waiting for it to air on MTV, I had nothing much to do, no job to go to and a tiny little bit of money left over from my payment for the show, so there seemed to be only one logical thing to do... go to Magaluf.

Jordan was by now officially my live-in boyfriend and he was going off to rep there, so I went along and we ended up staying there for a month. We lived in hotels when we could afford it, but mostly we lived like tramps because we barely had a penny between us.

I was making a tiny bit of money as a shot girl along the strip – handing out free shots in the hope of getting people into bars – while Jordan sold tickets and enjoyed himself. He kept telling everyone, 'She's going to be in *Ex on the Beach*,' like it was some massive thing.

I liked him enough to hang out with him, but he was a little bit of a twat. He did like to tell porkies about girls, and sometimes he couldn't help but big himself up, which meant I got the wrong idea about situations. This often turned into more bust-ups in bars. I still hadn't learned the lessons of Nu Bar – stay sober, don't get into rows, don't always blame the other girl – and if I'm honest, even these Magaluf scraps were still all about The Dip.

I could switch in a flash, and for some reason I didn't care how I came across in public. Sober, I was quietly spoken, always polite, remembering the good manners my parents and grandparents had taught me. Drunk, I could say vile, disgusting things without even thinking about it. I'd always been a quiet thing, a small girl who never stood up for myself. Now, if I ever felt remotely threatened by someone – which was often – I wouldn't hold back and I'd just be rude to them, often before they even said anything. Looking back, it was like I was discovering my voice, finding out I could actually hold my own.

My targets weren't any of this lot in Magaluf either. It was actually those pricks who'd been horrible to me all those previous years, but it was only now coming out of me. Now, in bars, on the strip, down at the beach, it didn't matter where, if somebody said something I took the wrong way, I was having none of it. I would jump down their throat and not even give them a chance to explain. Girls were scared of me, while some boys quite liked this unpredictable creature. But both girls and guys were wary of me, and they were right to be.

Did I like this new Megan? Well, I knew deep down that I was still very unhappy and I was putting on a front, but at least I felt strong now, able to protect myself. So that all worked, in public at least. It was only when I went home that I was crying, carrying on drinking, abusing my body like crazy.

Ex on the Beach finally came out, and, overnight, I became this person who everybody on Twitter wanted to follow. Every evening the show aired, my followers went up, by tens of thousands. Then, the really bad stuff started appearing on the show, but every time I had a meltdown, more and more people started following me on social media.

In the street, girls started coming up to me, and these were proper rude, scary girls that normally I'd run away from myself. Instead, it was them seeking me out and saying, 'Oi Megan, you're sweet, mate.' I thought, 'What's going on here?' I think I was saying stuff they wished they could say themselves, so they could relate to that person they saw on screen.

So I kept it all going. I started being funny but also lairy on social media, and then I got another call from MTV, saying they were about to start casting the next series of *Ex on the Beach*.

'Do you want to come back? We're going to make a big deal of it if you do.'

I wasn't sure about going back on. But, after all those years of auditions, of trying to get my name and face out there, it felt like things were finally starting to take off for me. I'd signed with an agent, I was getting offers of public appearances, a bit more money this time, plus they said I could go back on the show with Jordan.

So I agreed, and the next thing I knew, they'd made a whole separate advert with my face coming out of the water. They tagged it 'Armeganeddon'. I thought, 'Well something's obviously working. I won't change a thing.'

Turned out I didn't have to. If them producers wanted me to kick off as usual, they chose the perfect person to put in front of me, but once again it looked as though I was being entirely irrational, losing my shit for no apparent reason. Well, let me tell my side of the story, and I'll leave you to judge for yourself whether there was no apparent reason...

First, what did the viewers get to see? Well, me and Jordan arrived out of the sea in episode four, halfway through the series. In the previous series, we'd both had our turn sitting on the beach waiting for the possibility of an ex to arrive, so we knew how terrifying it was. But it was equally terrifying, walking up the beach, turning up new and not knowing what kind of reception you're going to get.

Scotty T from *Geordie Shore* was sat there with a couple of girls. As soon as we got to them, one of the girls jumped up and hugged Jordan, so it was clear she knew him. I said on camera, 'Fuck me, Jordan's been scraping the barrel. Four out of ten, mate,' which I know sounds a bit bitchy. Later that evening, I upped my game and I said to her, 'Daddy's little princess, did he buy you a boob job too?' Equally nasty, but hopefully you'll understand in a minute.

The next day, we all went off to a water park, and I was enjoying myself, hanging out with the girls until I spotted Jordan deep in chat with this same girl on a balcony. This was shit for me to see, but I soon made it known, screaming at him – Mental Megs came back out to play.

It definitely would have looked like I was taking something out on this girl for no reason, but nobody realised what was really going on behind the scenes.

Before we went back on the show, I said to Jordan, 'Have you done anything that would upset me if they drag it up on the show? Because you know they WILL drag it up.' He said to me, with a completely straight face, 'No, Megan, you have nothing to worry about.'

Then, when we were walking up the beach just ahead of filming, I asked him again, but there was still nothing, apparently. Then the producers gave me a big sambuca and told me, 'One of Jordan's exes is on the beach.' They told me her name, and I asked Jordan, 'Who is this girl?' He said, 'I just fucked her once.' Obviously any girl would want to know a bit more.

He then added a final point. The pair of us had been to a club only the previous week, and it turned out it belonged to this girl's dad. We were getting further and further up the beach while this chat was going on, getting ready to make our debut on this series. At this point, we could see Scotty T and the other two girls, and even Jordan looked a bit sheepish. We'd had a group of girls dancing and standing on our table at the club the week before, and it turned out she'd been one of them girls. By now I was four sambucas down, so I was tipsy, and I couldn't believe he'd taken me to the club of one of his shags – where we'd had a great night, drunk loads of their vodka – and he'd forgotten to mention it. 'I didn't think she'd be on the show, Megan,' was his reasoning. Did this muppet have no idea how the industry works? Girls LOVE having one up on each other. Of course she was going to be here. Just as we got to them on the beach, he added, 'She won't say anything, she won't say anything.' As if.

The first thing she said to me was, 'Enjoy the vodka, did you?' and that was it. 'Enjoy living off Daddy's money, do you?' I replied, and off we went. At the end of the day, she hadn't done anything wrong – as usual, the other girl hadn't actually committed a crime, it was just easier for me to think she had – but she clearly enjoyed having one over me, as predicted. So we kicked off. It was all a bit dramatic – our drinks ended up all over each other and we had to be pulled apart. The producers were all buzzing. I was genuinely fuming about the whole thing – I hate being mugged off, probably because I've been mugged off so much in the past, but I think I also felt the pressure of living up to the whole 'Mental Megs' thing, even though I tried to dodge it, and the producers kept stirring it up. They definitely encouraged me to be bitchier than I would have been normally – I called one girl 'Harry Potter' just because she had glasses. I think by then I was just a bit bored. Sorry, Kristina.

During that series, which was luckily shorter than the previous one, and filmed in Portugal, we had all the usual dramas. I was sent on a date with another boy called Lewis, and he tried his luck with me. It turned out this boy, who'd been going on all the way through about the importance of having respect for women, suddenly saw nothing wrong in trying it on with someone else's girlfriend. We had to go on this shit painting date, and at one point he turned to me and said, 'You and I are going to get married.' I didn't like that. Then he asked if he had a chance. Well, I hated that. I told him, 'Never,' then went back to the villa and told Jordan. On that occasion, Jordan actually grew some balls for once and went and said something. Lewis kicked off big time – he started waving his arms around, had to be put on the floor by security and ended up actually being chucked off the show. Just another day on *Ex on the Beach*!

But the real problem for me in that house was the other girls.

They'd all clearly been watching me on the other series, and they'd worked out that if they behaved as nutty as me, they'd get the same amount of attention. So they all took turns to behave as if they were out of control, but I knew they were putting it on, while I was still being genuine. Everyone was pretending to be the big, mouthy one, but I didn't have to pretend. If someone pisses me off, it shows all over my face – I've never had to fake it, and I think viewers and other people can tell the difference.

There was one girl in particular who made it a horrible experience for me. Some of the other girls had warmed to me by then, but she led a little clique giving those girls a hard time for it. Jordan and I turned up late to the show, so the friendship groups had already been formed. Yet again, it was like being back at Woodbridge. I was in the house for two weeks and they felt like the longest two weeks of my life. Although we looked quite happy on camera, Jordan and I actually rowed the whole time we were there, and the producers were hoping for a big argument to kick off between this particular girl and me. Eventually they got it. They created competition between us with a talent show one evening, both of us singing, both of us already on the sambuca – what could go wrong?

She'd been upstairs practising; she was all ready to give her best Alicia Keys impression, and she didn't like it when I belted out a tune. We'd been grating on each other for days, but the fight really came out of nowhere. She called Jordan good-looking but then she said, 'I don't find your man attractive.' I told her I didn't need the attitude, and she took her glasses off and threw them. For once, it was actually me thinking, 'What just happened? Calm the fuck down.' That didn't last long, though. She put out her hand, I shoved it away, she got me in a headlock, and we were at each other. Next thing I knew, I was being marched off by security and screaming, 'She thinks she's the big girl in here, well she ain't the big girl. I'm the fucking big girl.' Once again, I had completely lost it.

I was furious with her, but I was also upset at the producers, screaming at them, 'How could you put me in this situation, twisting it and then allowing her to carry on?'

It wasn't unusual for me to lose my shit, but this time, I couldn't seem to calm down. Not to play a broken record, but once again it was that all-too-familiar feeling of being bullied, of someone trying to have one over me and trying to make me feel small. I wasn't an angel and I knew we were all supposed to have a good row from time to time and make good telly, but I wasn't in there to get this hurt.

Because I was still raging, I got taken to stay in the villa next door. I was absolutely beside myself – lying on the floor, screaming and packing my clothes to go home. I couldn't get control of myself, and I was somewhere where no one cared about me. I just wanted to get out of there.

Looking back on that now makes me feel sad. I realised I needed counselling, and I needed to go home. The producers told me to sleep on it. They even let me call home, and I spoke to my mum really briefly. She didn't say much, just told me to come home if I thought I had to.

The next morning, I got taken for a chat with a really senior producer. She sat me down and said, 'Listen to me. Do you want to be a star?' I realised this wasn't the average pep talk they gave everyone, so I replied honestly: 'I want to make something of myself.'

She said, 'Do yourself a favour, go back in that villa and hold your head high. Apologise to the girl for shoving her first, because you did. I think you should do it, because I have a feeling other TV opportunities could come your way.'

I asked, 'What, really?'

She said, 'Yes.'

Okay, then. I put a smile on my face, went back in the house and apologised to the girl. She did too. We hated each other, but at least we shook on it, and we just avoided each other after that. I made myself feel better by saying on camera, 'As soon as I'm home, I'm blocking that bitch on Twitter.' Later on, that same girl kicked off again with someone completely different. See, it's not just me.

The next day happened to be my birthday. It was right near the end of our stay in the villa, so Jordan 'hosted' a big party for me. All the food was gluten-free and everyone was wearing a paper crown. Jordan had already given me a toy elephant and a nice card in the morning, but I didn't realise he still had something else up his sleeve.

We went upstairs to the penthouse, where Jordan suddenly got down on one knee, pulled out a ring and proposed. Actually asked me to marry him! What the fucking fuck? So there I was, paralytic, with a glass of Prosecco in my hand, staring at a grinning boy in tight white jeans, both of us wearing paper crowns, taking part in a TV reality show, with rose petals on the bed and cameras rolling next to us. Of course I said, 'Yes.'

It was strangely emotional. I think I was just happy that a boy was being nice to me. Jordan told me I deserved to be happy because, as he put it, 'You've been treated like shit so much.' He was loving the 'tamed man' thing, and the ring he bought me was quite sweet. Jordan told me he'd spent £500 on it. Every time he mentioned it when the show aired, the real price popped up on screen – '£179'. Like how stupid could he be? Did he really think the producers were going to keep that a secret for him?

right:
Getting
ready for
Nubar.
God, I look
a state!

above: My first night out ... Movida!

right:
Me and
Lauren
loving
Nubar!

above: **Me aged 19 with Harry in Nubar**

below: **Me at Nubar Xmas party**

above: **Me being a table host at Nubar**

right: **Me and Jordan**

left: Entering *CBB*

below: Losing my shit and being taken out of the *CBB* house by security

Not in here

left: Moaning about my clothes being thrown in the pool

right: Apologising the next day to Big Brother ...

below: Spending the night away from the main house. I was not happy.

right: Me and Gem

below: My eviction night and finale!

above: **Singing for MTV in Covent Garden**

above and left: **Me entering** *TOWIE* **for the first time**

left: Me and Chloe before our fall-out

below: Another drama at Sugar Hut

After the big proposal and my acceptance, he said, 'I need to ring your mum and dad about this.' I got a bit cross, asking him, 'What do you mean, you haven't rung them?' and being all old-fashioned about it, even though inside I was thinking, 'This isn't real.' But I knew it was all going to be on TV, so they had to know first.

Jordan dialled my mum's number, and I heard him say, 'Tanya, can I speak to you about something?' I was meant to be standing outside our room, but I could hear their chat easily. He seemed to go a bit weird and just said, 'Okay then, bye.' I knew my mum and dad really liked him – I mean they knew he was a bit of a bean but they still liked him – but he told me my mum had said, 'Sorry, Jordan, it's not a good time to talk.' I knew that was really out of character for my mum, so I insisted on calling her myself. We weren't allowed any phones in the villa, but the producers made an exception for me on this occasion. I think they already had an inkling of what was going on at home. By the time I dialled the number, if I'm honest, so did I. Because for the previous two nights, I'd been having some very strange dreams...

15

My granddad will always be one of the great loves of my life. He's the reason, along with my mum, that I have belief in myself. When I was little, both of them would get cross with me whenever I used to get down and say, about my dreams of performing, 'It's not going to happen.' My mum would say, 'Never say that,' and my granddad was the same. He always told me, 'You're going to make it, Megan.'

The whole time I was growing up, I sang for my granddad, I performed little routines for him in the garden with him sat in his chair, and of course we had our fishing. Even as I got older and started going out, I went over to see him all the time and told him everything I was up to. He would even find me good songs to cover. I couldn't have asked for a better person in my life, but now he was really ill, and it was breaking my heart.

Between the two series of *Ex on the Beach*, I was spending every single day with my granddad, who we all silently knew was on his last legs. When I started getting shit in the press for my meltdowns during the first series, what nobody realised was that I was spending all my time sharing caring duties with the other members of my family. On the one hand, all that negative press could have made things worse, but really, because I was so worried about my granddad, it meant I wasn't really worrying about any of that other stuff.

He was fading fast, and, as well as having us to look after him, he had palliative care with him every day. A few months before, my nan had gone out shopping with some friends, which was a rare occasion by now as she didn't like to leave him, when he phoned my mum and said, 'I think I'm having a heart attack.' My mum called me as she was on her way back home from work, and said, 'You need to get there asap.' I was sitting eating my lunch, and I literally threw my plate in the air, got in the car and raced down the wrong side of the road as the traffic was so bad, just because I knew I had to get to my granddad over in Chingford. I could see cars coming at me, people bibbing their horns, but I kept thinking, 'He's going to die, he's going to die.'

I finally got over there, and he was sitting in a chair in the kitchen. I got on the phone to emergency services, and they told me what to do until they turned up, which they finally did. It felt like forever, even though it was probably only a few minutes, and I watched them take him away in the ambulance. Once we got to the hospital, he was in a bad way, and we all stood round the bed, while they put defibrillator pads on him to regulate his heartbeat. The whole thing was terrifying. They got him going again and kept him in hospital, but that was really the beginning of the end.

We knew he was dying, and we were all beside ourselves. Around this time, there was talk of me going back on *Ex on the Beach* for the next series, and I had no idea whether I should go or not. My granddad started to fade quite quickly after that. Once he got home again, the Marie Curie palliative care team came in – they were amazing, I'll never be able to say enough good things about them – and our whole family were with him every day. I recorded a song, which we played to him while we sat in his room hour after hour. We all took turns helping him sit up. It was a terrible time.

He had Parkinson's disease, so he could no longer speak or swallow, but he used to tap out words on his little pad. He kept writing to me, 'You're going to be a star.' I told him about the offers of more TV, and showed him the clips from the first series that I could get away with. He didn't like me rowing with people, and he used to say, 'That isn't the Megan I know.' He knew it was because I'd been hurt by my previous ex. So we had to be careful what we showed him – there I was singing and smiling, nothing of me throwing plates around and swearing on national television. But he said he knew that wasn't going to be my line of work, he knew the singing was what I really wanted to do – that was always my dream.

He tapped out that he wanted me to go back for the second series. I kept asking him if he was sure. He said he wouldn't be happy, thinking I was stopping for him. He wrote, 'Don't stop, you go.'

It was definitely one of the hardest moments of my life when I left his room, having made the decision to go, and I'll never forget that moment. I told him I'd see him later, and I really didn't think he was going to die, but I did have a massive lump in my throat as I said goodbye. I knew I had to fulfil his wishes. It would have upset him even more if I'd stayed. I said goodbye, went to the door and took one last look back. I was so frightened that it might be the last time we saw each other, and that's what it turned out to be.

The whole two weeks before I went into the villa, I had terrible dreams every night. One of my constant nightmares was that I was driving my car, with my granddad sat next to me, dead. I told my mum about it and she said, 'It's because you know he's on his way.'

Two nights before the end of the show, I woke up in the middle of the night. I woke Jordan as well and told him,

'I've had a really weird dream. My granddad was there and he was laughing.' All those previous dreams, he'd been dead, but now here he was laughing.

The following evening was when we got engaged at my birthday party. We were in the penthouse suite, and in the middle of the night, I woke up with a light shining from the corner of the room, where the cameras were. I thought it was the nightlight, but it seemed a bit bright and I carried on staring at it. I suddenly realised it was the wrong corner to be a camera, and I can only say now that I felt something in the room.

I woke Jordan up again, and told him I felt freaked out. I said, 'My granddad was just talking to me, and it was pure white in this dream.'

In the dream, we were in some place that I can't explain – it was just me and him, and he looked like he did all those years before, when we used to visit the chalet. He had his glasses on, he was wearing his jumper and he had a big, fat belly. By the time he was ill, he was skin and bones, but he'd been much bigger before. In the dream, he was laughing about his teeth. It was the one thing he used to moan about during his illness – he hardly ever complained, but he hated not having his teeth in, and now here he was laughing, saying, 'My teeth, my teeth.' He had his jumper on and his teeth in. I said, 'Granddad, you're laughing,' and we had a proper conversation. He kept reassuring me, saying he wasn't in pain, and then he wandered off and... that's when I woke up with the light. Now I genuinely believe that was my granddad making his proper goodbye to me.

He'd actually died two nights before, that stupid evening when I'd got into the fight with that girl, when security had taken me out and had me moved to the next villa. It was the night I'd rung my mum because I'd been beside myself and wanted to come home, but she didn't want to tell me on the phone, as he'd already passed, and she knew he wanted me to do well.

After Jordan had proposed and rung my parents to be told, 'It's not a good time,' I phoned and asked what was going on. My mum just said that she was busy with work. I even tried to get her to talk to Jordan, but she wouldn't. Then I asked her, 'Is everything all right?' She said it was. I asked, 'Is Granddad all right?' She said he was fine. I said, 'Well, I think he was just here with me.'

My mum and nan were both on the line to me, and there was a silence before they both became hysterical on the phone, almost like a scream, and they didn't have to say anything else, because I knew. They couldn't believe he'd somehow come to me in Portugal, but they felt reassured by it, and we all cried together on the phone. I'll never forget hearing that.

Once again in that villa, I was beside myself, on the floor sobbing. Then the producers decided it was time for me to go.

Jordan came with me and I took the engagement ring off. I told him, 'I know you want this, but it just seems wrong.' I knew that if I really loved him, if we were meant to be together, then even at that worst moment in my life, it would have been a comfort having him there, it would have been a positive thing, and it just wasn't. So I took the ring off and said, 'We don't talk about this any more.' We agreed that if we really wanted to get engaged, we needed to talk about it properly, but there was no rush.

There was meant to be a week-long shoot afterwards – odd bits of filming to finish everything off – but I was in a hurry to get home, so I did the first lot of photos the very next morning and got the first flight home. I was back home as soon as it was feasibly possible, but it killed me that I hadn't been there for my granddad at the end.

If I hadn't gone away and done the second series, there would have been no *Celebrity Big Brother*, no *TOWIE* and no singing, so it was only by doing what my granddad asked and leaving him behind that his dream for me started coming true. He always told me, 'Everything happens for a reason, Megan,' and I do believe that, but the timing was terrible, and it will always be heartbreaking.

16

When we got back home, Jordan and I – surprise, surprise – weren't really getting on. *Ibiza Weekender* aired and I started getting sent tweets hinting he was up to no good out there. He never admitted to anything, and I believe he was genuinely in love with me, but he was so young, he didn't really know how to behave, and I was starting to do my own thing.

The things I had to deal with in my life at that point were starting to be grown-up ones – looking for a flat, sorting out my career, dealing with our family's bereavement – and he was still a little child, really. He didn't have his own home, he was still living with us, and he was loving all the attention *Ex on the Beach* had brought us both.

Why did I accept his proposal? I can see now I
wasn't in love with him, and I think I knew it then, but my
acceptance of the whole thing does sort of give you an
indication of what happens to you when you enter one of
these reality TV shows for any length of time. You have to
be really strong and really careful, and, if I'm honest, I was
neither one of those.

I'm not the first person to say that it's not like real life
in there. You're in this little bubble – you have no phone,
no access to your real friends who actually care about you,
and you get told what time to get up, when to go out and
who to go out with. As a result, you end up getting really
close to the other people in there, just because you're with
them every hour of the day, every day, and that becomes
your life.

I did have a really good time with Jordan, but it wasn't
real, and I probably gave it far more time and attention
than I would have done in the real world. Back here, I'd
have just carried on being heartbroken about The Dip, and
eventually got over it. Jordan wouldn't have been in the
picture. Instead, in there – with producers winding you up,
everyone else winding you up – your judgement goes out
the window. Or mine did, at least. So by the time he did
the whole proposing thing, it just seemed like one more
unreal thing.

What was I going to say on national television to
my nice boyfriend, who'd been living with my family for

months? It was a very difficult situation for me and I felt a lot of pressure, but I knew deep down getting engaged was wrong. When he lied about the price of the ring, well that just summed up the entire situation for me – I realised it had all got a bit out of control, and it was time to rein it back in. By then, Jordan was getting carried away by all the airtime – like a lot of other people I know, he absolutely thrives on all of it – but I know that when it matters, I'm real.

So guess what? Jordan and I broke up. Not the biggest shocker you've read so far, I bet, but it was exhausting all the same. It involved breaking up, getting back together, then breaking up again for about three weeks before we actually called it quits, and it became really tiring, because he was such a liar.

At one point, he went off to film something called *Release the Hounds*, and his ex-fling – yes, ANOTHER previous fling – went on it with him. I said to Jordan before he went how on edge I felt about her being there; I said, 'I don't want any flirting behaviour.' Is that a lot to ask of someone you're in a relationship with, when they're even living with you in your family home?

He said, 'Don't worry, Megan,' and off he went to film. When he got back, I asked him, 'Is there going to be anything on the show I don't like?' Of course he said that there was nothing to worry about, that it was all fine.

And then I saw the ad – which was him and the girl being too close for my liking. The one thing I'd asked him not to do, he'd done. And the ad was one or two seconds long – what was the actual show going to be like? Typical Jordan – it was just like walking up that beach again.

I'd had enough, and I thought at that point, 'Nope, you're out.' I started to pack his bags and put them in his car. He'd been living with my family for six months – rent-free, may I add. When he came back, I didn't even let him in the house. Instead, I waited for him to come back, opened the door, gave him his car key and shut the door again, telling him, 'We're done.' His whole body went red in panic, but I was completely over it. If I'm honest, I had been for a while.

Off he went, until he came back a while later. He'd been staying at his mate's place, and we met in his car. He begged me to take him back, saying he'd changed and all that bollocks. But I said no, and that was the last time I saw him.

Jordan always claims that I dumped him in order to go on *Celebrity Big Brother*. That wasn't true, so I want to clear up once and for all exactly what happened.

Before we split up, I got the chance to go for an interview in London, just to have a chat about possibly going on *CBB* at some point in the future.

At that stage, it was literally only a discussion – I wasn't allowed to tell anybody because it all had to be kept totally secret, and, besides, I never like to tell anyone about stuff I'm going for. I don't like to get my hopes up in case it doesn't happen, and also I don't like to jinx things by talking about them. I've always been the same.

So I went for *CBB*, and during that initial chat, the producers knew I was with Jordan and that I could possibly be in a relationship during my time on the show, if I ended up going in the house. However, they knew and I knew that they wanted me in there for one reason and one reason only – they wanted the lunatic I'd shown myself to be on *Ex on the Beach*.

So when I got back from my meeting, I didn't feel the need to say anything to Jordan – there was nothing definite to say, plus I'd been sworn to secrecy and I didn't want to blow my chances.

One of the producers knew Jordan, and not long after this first meeting, they told him I'd been for an interview. I still hadn't told him, plus it was made more awkward because I knew he had his own heart set on appearing in *CBB*. It can start to get awkward when you're both going for the same things, so when he asked me, I said, truthfully, 'I've been for an interview but that's it. It's early stages.' He was really angry, saying, 'I can't believe you didn't tell me.' But there was nothing to tell. I'd been for a meeting but that was it.

He didn't take that very well, but then we had all the *Release the Hounds* shit and we broke up anyway.

Soon after that, my manager called me and said, 'Are you sitting down? You've got *CBB*.' I replied, 'No I don't. You're joking? Surely I haven't got this? I don't believe it.'

Then it hit me. I was jumping up and down and screaming. I literally couldn't believe it. Plus, by sheer chance, it was going to be on screen on Channel 5, while *Ex on the Beach* was going out on MTV. Megan McKenna, coming to you from Essex, on two channels at the same time.

So, despite what Jordan says, there was no fib, there was no intention to get rid of him in time for my big debut on *CBB*, it was just a random bit of timing, which meant that when I went into the house, I was completely single and ready to go.

As I was walking up the steps in my long, blue dress, I remember standing behind the Big Brother Eye and seeing the audience through the tiny gap that was about to open up and reveal me.

I could hear my VT playing and the whole crowd was booing. I remember turning to the right, looking at one of the producers and saying, 'I'm terrified. They all hate me,' and he said, 'You'll be fine.'

The next minute I heard my name being called by Emma Willis, and the doors opened to thousands of people and cameras flashing and screaming at me. These weren't good screams, though. People were not keen.

It's fair to say I wasn't mentally prepared for everything that was coming my way. A lot had gone on over the past couple of years – I was still coming to terms with all the heartache I'd gone through with The Dip, and Jordan's fibs hadn't exactly helped heal those wounds. By now, I was getting a lot of attention, both positive and negative, on social media and sometimes in the street, which takes some getting used to. Most importantly, I was still grieving heavily for my granddad – he'd left a massive gap in my family's lives, and I could get emotional very easily. Looking back, I probably wasn't in the right frame of mind to take part in these shows.

During that series, it was the usual crazy mix of people – some a bit past their heyday and others on the way up. We had David Bowie's ex-wife Angie, *X Factor* contestant Christopher Maloney, former *EastEnders* actors Danniella Westbrook and John Partridge, *Hollyoaks* actress Stephanie Davis, actor Darren Day, Liza Minelli's ex-husband David Gest, dancer Kristina Rihanoff, ex-WAG Nancy Dell'Olio, a political activist called Winston McKenzie and Kim Kardashian's best friend Jonathan Cheban. There were also the usual bunch of reality stars like Jeremy McConnell, an American girl called Tiffany Pollard, *TOWIE*'s Gemma Collins and a face I recognised straight away from *Ex on the Beach*, Scotty T.

I went into the house with boos from the crowd – pretty much what I expected, because of my famous meltdowns on *Ex on the Beach* – but that wasn't what I was actually most worried about.

I was actually a lot more nervous about what was going to go on inside the house. My legs were like jelly as I walked in, but I seemed to get on all right with everyone. I felt a bit shy at first, especially with some of the familiar older faces in there, and some of the older people seemed to be looking down on me as though I wasn't good enough to be in there.

I got on with the majority of people in there. I loved Gemma, Danniella, Darren Day and David Gest. Only a few months later, I was really sad when I heard David had died. He was such a lovely man and he was really nice about my singing voice.

My crowd in there almost instantly became Jeremy, Scotty, Stephanie and Jonathan. Jonathan was a bit older, but he liked to come and join in too.

Stephanie and I talked a lot during our time together in the house. I heard all about her stuff going on – she asked for loads of advice about her boyfriend on the outside, plus what she should do about Jeremy, who she fancied on the inside. She ignored all my advice, but she knew I'd just been through a breakup with Jordan, so we shared a lot of stories. Sound familiar? Too right. During her time in the house, she said about me, 'I love her to bits. She's my sister for life.' Well, that didn't last long. We met up once after we left. I know things went really downhill with her and Jeremy, but he was still a good friend of mine. Then one day I got tagged in an article – she'd been pictured kissing Jordan on a night out. I was completely baffled about why she would do that, and I still don't know to this day. I just thought, 'They're as bad as each other.'

Meanwhile, back in the *Big Brother* house, as soon as we got settled down in there, it seemed like Scotty T fancied me a bit. Scotty's reputation wasn't the best, and don't forget I'd seen his antics close up during our time on *Ex on the Beach*. But he was funny and seemed like a laugh, and I thought, 'Fuck it, I'm single.' It was no big deal – we were just in there together and it was like a holiday romance. Besides, a little kiss here and there never hurt anyone, did it? I just knew I didn't want any more aggro. He was very charming, had this big smirk and I just genuinely liked him as a person. When we all came out, we were together at the party for the finale, and then I never saw him again. No story, and, as I'd hoped, absolute zero aggro. All told, one of my healthiest ever relationships.

I had a good time in the *CBB* house. It was an amazing experience, but, I have to say, it was also one of the hardest TV things I've ever had to do. As the days went on, I got more and more hungry and tired. Everyone was snoring, which made it really difficult to get any sleep, and it's amazing how the little things can start winding you up in there – it's like being at school but never going home.

I remember lending Stephanie some clothes, and then finding them later on the floor. She'd been in the pool wearing them, and they were drenched. I ended up screaming my head off, 'No one's borrowing my stuff any more. No one's respecting my shit,' when I could probably have just said, 'Could you pick it up, please?' I'd officially lost it, but I know if that was me, I wouldn't have done that.

Later, I saw Jeremy folding Steph's clothes, and, instead of ignoring it, I screamed at him, 'She needs to clean her own shit. It's a fucking normal thing. Clean your own fucking shit.' He was just being nice, but I was obviously starting to get sick of her ways, like you can do when you're around the same people twenty-four seven.

18

At the beginning of the second week, they gave us a task to do, so we had to act like puppets — which meant eating like puppets as well, apparently. I need my food or I get hungry. I'm skinny already, so not having any food makes me feel weak. (The food they gave us was like puppet food: really tiny portions.) We got given cold lentil soup and everyone was complaining, but having no food really got to me. One night, I went into the diary room to have a rant about the lentil soup, saying, 'I wouldn't give my dog that, it's sick on a plate.'

Another time, I was banging on the door of the diary room. I knew by now I was living up to my reputation as Mental Megs — one headline about the show was 'Megan has a meltdown over mashed potato' — but I was

142

so hungry, I didn't care. I was screaming, 'All I want is a fucking piece of toast. I'm starving.' I was trying to explain that it was because of my gastric problems, but I couldn't get the words out, and all I could see were people smiling and laughing at me getting upset. Stephanie literally fell to the floor laughing over what she saw as my usual over-reaction. It was me and food, as always, only this time, because of the task, I was still wearing a black T-shirt and a pink, spotty bow tie. I was screaming at the Big Brother camera, ranting about them feeding me 'three crackers and a fucking fig'. I didn't even know what a bloody fig was but it was vile.

When I came back from the diary room, instead of any food, we'd been given massive bottles of Strongbow, tins of Spam and packets of Smash. It was literally like eating what I imagine cat food tastes like. As hungry as I was, I couldn't force it down my mouth, so Scotty ended up eating my Spam. Of course, I drank the Strongbow, and went to bed on an empty tummy – not a good move!

The next day, we had a party to celebrate the end of the task. More drink was flowing, only this time it was wine, vodka and some Prosecco. I think it's fair to say I was backing it. On an empty stomach, after not eating for two days, it's also fair to say it got to me. Once again, I was completely paralytic.

I walked into the bedroom and heard John Partridge slagging off Stephanie, and this is when things started to go very wrong. It seemed to me like John was playing a game while he was in there, pretending to be all calm and mature, but playing people off against each other the whole time. My intentions all came from a good place, but because I was so drunk, everything I said came out all the wrong way. I was trying to get him to stop bitching about her – I kept saying he should just talk to her instead. It was some crap about her not tidying up her clothes. For a while, I had people agreeing with me, with Gemma saying, 'Megan's right, stop bitching.'

I should have stopped right there, but I was feeling paranoid about being judged for drinking too much, so I carried on shouting. At one point, I screamed at the top of my voice, 'I clean my shit up. If I want a fucking drink, I can have a fucking drink. End of.'

All I wanted to say to John was, 'If you want to say something, pull her in here and tell her to her face.' I kept saying, 'Tell her, tell her to clean her shit up,' but because I was so fucked, the psycho in me soon came out. What was behind it? Hunger, being drunk, breakups, lies, the whole shitty shebang. I would not stop shouting, despite everyone trying to calm me down. Even gentle David tried, but I wasn't listening to anyone.

Then, somewhere in the corner of my eye, I noticed Tiffany in the room, sitting in bed, laughing. I had no problem at all with her, we actually really got on, but I said to her, 'I don't know why you're laughing, Tiffany, he's the one who wanted everyone to walk out of this house for you! I stood up for you!'

It was true, that's exactly what he'd been doing. A couple of days before, John had said he felt uncomfortable in the house and he thought she shouldn't be here, and he'd tried to start a petition for us to all walk out of the house.

Because I didn't think it was fair, I told her. But because I was so drunk and beyond all control, I shouted it at her really aggressively, so jumbled up that she couldn't even listen to the words coming out of my mouth, she just heard me screaming. And she got up and went for me. Gemma was holding me back and... well, yep, it was just like Nu Bar all over again, except this time on national television.

What was really going on? I was trying to get my point across, but it wasn't to her, it wasn't to anyone else in the room, it was about John being a bully and me hating what he was doing and trying to stand up to him. He was so in control of the situation – he knew exactly what he was doing, and he was loving it. He just sat there, saying, 'Oh look, look,' and then Kristina joined in, laughing.

Everyone was saying, 'Look at her,' which wound me up even more. By now, I was completely out of control, hysterical – everything the producers had hoped for in booking me – and my gang had to restrain me and pull me into the bathroom. By now, my eyes were like the Devil's and I was literally foaming at the mouth. My problem was with John, so I shouted, 'He plays a game. He acts like a fucking innocent little shit bag. He stands there and acts like Mr Innocent. Fuck off, you little c**t. You don't give a shit about anyone apart from yourself... I'll go sick on that c**t. Do not lie on that bed and look at me with your fucking eyebrows pointing at me like that.' Finally, the punchline, when it came, was short and sweet: 'I've eaten gruel for that c**t.' It's fair to say it was defo not my finest hour.

That was when the voice of Big Brother boomed out, telling me to go to the diary room, but by then I couldn't even speak. I have absolutely no memory of being in that bathroom, saying what I was saying. My conscious side had blanked out, while my nutty side had kicked in. All I knew was that, once again, I felt trapped in a bubble with no one who really cared for me.

I then had to go to the diary room, which was fine until I heard the sound of the lock turn. They'd actually locked me in, which was the worst thing they could possibly have done. With me, when I'm in a situation that's got all confused like that, all I want to do is sort it out straight away. I don't want to go and beat someone up, I just want to sort out any misunderstandings, and that's what I wanted then, because I knew it had gone to a level that was bad – what I didn't realise then was just how bad. I became so frustrated, I even hit the camera at one point. Then security turned up and started asking me what had happened, and that's when things went from bad to worse.

I was still feeling really upset, pointing out that they'd let Tiffany off for bad behaviour, but now they were going for me. I hadn't attacked anyone, I was never going to – look at me, I know I'm a twig in clothes – but they thought I was planning to go back in and smash the gaff up. I got more and more frustrated, shouting, 'You let Tiffany get away with everything.' I was a drunk mess. My anger was actually directed entirely at John Partridge, never her, but I was so angry, everything spilled out in the wrong way.

Just my luck, I got put in a different room for the night – all it had was a bed and a toilet, like a prison cell. I was desperate to go home, and asked to speak to the psychologist, but I finally passed out.

I woke up the next morning, by now feeling like complete shit with a massive hangover. They told me to go back into the diary room and asked me if I remembered what I'd said the night before. I couldn't, so they went through it all, and it was terrible. When I heard the words read back to me right there and then once I was sober, I was gutted that I'd let myself get to that point, and that all my thoughts had come out so wrong. I had no idea what the outcome was going to be, and I had no idea this meltdown had gone viral out in the real world. I found out later that I was on the front cover of loads of national newspapers, people like Alan Carr were tweeting about me, it was being discussed on breakfast TV shows, you name it. I even ended up being the answer to a question on *The Chase*. It was only then I thought, 'Shit, I've actually made it.'

I knew I needed to go back inside and explain to Tiffany why I was actually rowing with John in the first place. I went straight back into the main room, found her, ignored the others, and managed to explain what had gone on, that it had been John meddling. Straight away, she said, 'Girl, come here,' and gave me a big hug, and then everything was sweet between us, as it had been before and stayed being after. I ended up with a formal warning, and Tiffany also got a warning, so we settled for that. As for John, I managed to avoid him mostly afterwards, although, when we did bump into each other, we were civil. Everything in the house seemed to calm down quite dramatically after that huge scene, actually. I was much more chilled out, and it was actually Gemma who started clashing with John more than I did. Clearly, he just doesn't understand us Essex girls.

However, I don't believe it was any coincidence that, a few days later, he nominated me for eviction – I left, still holding onto my dignity, on day eighteen. I could tell John wanted to win, and I like to think the audience saw through him and his calculating ways – cool head, cold heart. He eventually came sixth, and he said afterwards he'd learnt a lot in there. I agreed with him when he said that every human emotion gets blown up once you get inside the house. I think ultimately people ended up agreeing with me about John, but not for the first or last time in my life, I know it was my poor delivery skills that let me down.

A bigger lesson, one I'm still learning, is about the negative backlash of my rages. During my exit interview, I was pretty mortified when they played back the film of my meltdown inside the diary room, and I knew I had to apologise for hitting the camera. I tried to explain what was going on in my head, but I knew the pictures were what people would remember. Whenever that's happened in my life, it's never been who I want to be. Like I said, I was brought up really well by a loving family who taught me all about good manners. I don't think I've ever been given a cup of tea without saying 'thank you'. The anger comes out when I'm trying to express myself, and I feel like everyone's trying to stop me, probably because they've realised I'm pissed and angry and they know I'm not doing myself any favours. I've had people constantly try and calm me down, when they shouldn't bother because then I feel trapped. I just need to be left alone to burn myself out like a spinning top, although in an ideal world, I'd never be in that state in the first place. Like I said, I'm still learning.

My biggest swallow-me-up moments

💋 When people thought I had six toes (I really don't)...

💋 ... Talking of toes, the time my fake big toenail pinged off at Sisu, Marbella (I've had a fake one ever since my real one came off)

💋 Watching myself back calling every single person a c**t during the first series of *Ex on the Beach*

💋 Realising *CBB* aired me saying, 'I think I'm going to get the shits' to the whole nation

💋 Setting off for my very first PA, getting to the airport and realising I've lost my passport

💋 The time I was really drunk, came home and fell on the floor with my legs open and fanny out, in front of all of Milly's friends

💋 The time I was foaming at the mouth during *CBB*

💋 Getting a 'No' in front of 4,000 people in Wembley Arena during the Six-Chair Challenge during *The X Factor*

💋 Knowing that, just before an important occasion — whether it's a hot date, an audition or a business meeting — there's every chance I'll get the shits

💋 The night after I got evicted from *CBB*, running out of Faces straight into MaccyD's and cutting my knee open — the night before my massive press debut, photo shoots and all!

💋 Every time I used to backcomb my hair so much I looked like a lollipop

💋 Doing a poo behind the sofa — to be fair, I was only a toddler!

19

Even before I went into the *Big Brother* house, my schedule changed overnight. I went from sitting at home, waiting for the phone to ring, to jumping out of bed, dashing to photo shoots and having constant meetings with my manager, Jade. Plus, a new thing had cropped up in my life – travelling to personal appearances all over the country.

On paper, being a reality TV star sounds very glam and like an easy life. You're getting invited to clubs for their opening nights. If there's a red carpet, you walk along it – you're shaking hands with everyone, posing for photographs and networking constantly. You can never switch off.

But if you do want to make it for yourself in the reality TV world, and you start doing well, all this stuff comes with a full-on schedule. I can remember travelling around the UK for three months, sleeping in the back of the car, getting ready in service stations and eating McDonald's every single day, as we never had enough time to go to restaurants and there was nowhere else to change. Don't get me wrong, I loved every single minute of this lifestyle, and I couldn't be more grateful that I've had these chances, but what bugs me is when people say, 'What work? You're just being filmed for a living.' No, I'm also working my arse off.

On one of these occasions before I went on *CBB*, I was booked to make a personal appearance at a club over in Northern Ireland. Everyone seemed a bit rowdy when we got there, and I went through all the usual of saying hi to as many people as possible, shaking hands and posing for pictures. There was a queue of people waiting for selfies outside the VIP bit, and I was leaning over so no one was left out. As I turned around and started to party, I suddenly felt a massive bang on my head. Turned out, someone had thrown a bottle at me. I was so shocked, I couldn't even tell if I was in pain or not until my head started throbbing and a lump started forming on the back of my head. It was really traumatic – I was in tears, saying, 'Get me out of here.' My manager Jade got me back to the hotel.

The next morning, we went straight to the airport, and I was still in pain with a big bump on my head. I was sitting in the departure lounge, feeling sorry for myself, when a guy with long hair and very blue eyes came up to me with a cup of tea in his hand, saying, 'I thought you could do with this.' I recognised him straight away. That'll be Mr Pete Wicks.

I already knew Pete a tiny bit by then. We used to follow each other on Twitter, and like each other's tweets and pictures and stuff. He just seemed to be like a nice Essex boy, on a similar road to me. He told me that I used to serve him in Nu Bar, but I don't remember that. He said I was a right moody fucker, ha ha.

He'd joined the cast of *TOWIE* the previous summer, but even without the show making his face familiar, he'd have stood out a mile with his big blue eyes, long hair and tattoos. I liked that he was a bit different from the average Essex boy. He was edgy and had an aura, a confidence about him, and he was a few years older than me, so he seemed quite wise. Away from the show, he seemed to be successful and hard-working, something I found interesting as a contrast to his pirate looks. In a nutshell, on that freezing cold morning in Northern Ireland, I was happy to see him. Plus, with a cup of tea in his hand, he clearly knew the way to my heart from the start.

We started texting and making vague arrangements to go out somewhere, but then I got the big call from *CBB* and had to delay things. I remember telling him, 'I've gone and got this job.' He sent nice tweets, all supportive,

above: **Me and Danni**

left: **Struttin' in Marbella**

below: **The famous fringe scene**

above: MCK Grill with the McKennnas – Tanya, Milly, me, Harry & Dave

left: Milly and Jordan (Bros GF)

below: Mum, Dad and me

above and left:
The big street row

left: TV Choice
Awards with Pete

below: The moment it came
out about the texting

right: Singing on the West End stage

below: Photo shoot in Nashville

right: Just being
a cowgirl

below: Me and
Alice and Baby
Steven the lamb

right: Megan and
Milly in Nashville

left: **Me and Gregg**

below: **My first shift at Bobby's**

below: **The famous Bluebird café, Nashville**

left: On *Loose Women*, belting out 'Fields of Gold'

below: Me and the *Full Monty* girlies!

the whole time I was in the house, which made me like him more.

Afterwards, we texted again, and one afternoon, it turned out we were both in the same part of London, so we arranged to go for 'a quick drink'. Famous last words. We ended up going to a club, got really drunk, stopped off for a Maccy D's and then he dropped me home. Pretty much the perfect first date.

We hadn't realised, but someone had taken a photo of us and put it on social media. Pete was relatively new to *TOWIE* – he'd only just been introduced to the show as a friend of James Lock – but a million people watch the show religiously. As we both realised at the time and then soon forgot, once you're on *TOWIE*, you can't get away with anything.

I'd actually already been in a meeting with the show's producers. There'd been a few discussions about me coming on the show – properly this time, not like with Lola – but then I'd been offered *CBB* so I'd gone for that instead.

By now, my best friend Chloe Meadows had joined the show, so when news of my date with Pete reached the *TOWIE* producers, it was only a matter of time before I ended up on the show as well. It was a bit of a surprise, as they've never had someone from another TV show going on there. They wanted to test me out to see how I fitted in with the rest of the TOWIE gang, so I was Pete's surprise date to the party for the hundredth episode. I was also there to back up Chloe. I went straight to the defence of Chloe and Courtney when they argued with the other girls, and all the fireworks went off exactly as the producers had wanted them to.

As soon as the episode aired, it was agreed that I would become a full-time cast member.

So that was how my *TOWIE* life began. I was on the show for eighteen months, but it felt like years, because I had so much drama. One thing after another kept happening, and I couldn't seem to get away from it. I just kept trying to remember what my granddad always said: 'Everything happens for a reason, Megan.'

Chloe Meadows and I had been mates for as long as I can remember – we'd been friends really since we were tiny. We went to the same primary school, where she was in the year above me, and we also both went to Woodbridge. She wasn't bullied like I was, but she disliked the place as much as I did, and she did exactly the same as me – left as soon as she could, and went to Ravenscourt. She was still in the year above me, but we used to travel together to and from Essex every day, so we got really close. There were five of us, but I got really close to Chloe. Then I went off to ArtsEd while she went to another theatre school, but we stayed best friends throughout that time. She was at my house a lot. She was there for my split with Mr First, and she was there during all my heartbreak over Mr Venezuela. It was Chloe sitting on my bed while I was in a state in my room, hanging off the curtains. She didn't know what to do with me, but she stayed put, which meant a lot. She saw me at my lowest, and I saw her go through some stuff, too. We were each other's shoulder to cry on.

Then she went off to Australia for a few years, which meant she missed the official low in my life – the time when I started working at Nu Bar and going out with The Dip. By the time she got back, she was seeing a very different Megan – fighting, drinking, generally being a mess – and she was one of the voices in my ear, begging me to pull myself together. I'm not sure she necessarily always made things better when I got in them fights – we'd both been to theatre school so between us we could make a drama out of pretty much anything – but we both stuck around. She was back and forth to Australia for a bit, and then I got her a job at Nu Bar as well, so she could make a few more friends around Essex.

Then I left my job, finally split up with The Dip and went off to film the first lot of *Ex on the Beach*. I was a lairy, loud Essex girl, perfect for *TOWIE*, but I was already on TV by then, under contract to MTV, with the *CBB* producers looking in my direction too, so *TOWIE* had to wait. In the meantime, they grabbed Chloe and a few of my other friends, and put them on screen. Chloe had done quite a few acting jobs herself – that was how she'd saved up to go to Australia. In fact, she was the girl on screen before *TOWIE* aired, doing all the bingo stuff. When she got on the show, I bigged it up on my social media, and then the whole time I was in the *CBB* house, she sent loads of tweets, asking people to support me. Back then, we definitely had each other's back.

When I came out of the *CBB* house – went in to the sound of boos, came out to the sound of cheers, thankfully – it was my mum and Chloe who stood waiting to greet me. That's how close we were before *TOWIE*, so I thought being on the show together would be really straightforward, just like an extension of our normal lives hanging out together. Looking back now, I realise that was a bit naïve.

A couple of months later, I was actually on *TOWIE* myself. I was Pete's new girl, but I was also there to back up Chloe. Girl Band was in full force.

20

Pretty much as soon as I joined the show, I realised the other girls were never going to take to me. Chloe's group were the new bunch and they were already being picked on, even before I got there. Can you guess what I'm going to say? Yep, you got it... it was indeed just like bloody Woodbridge all over again, where we were the new girls at school that no one liked. We were younger than them, I had a TV background so they probably thought I was up myself, and Chloe was my best mate. Easy targets.

Let's be clear, Girl Band existed way before *TOWIE*. There was me, Maddie, Amber, Chloe and, later on, Courtney. We were a tight group and we never let anybody get in the way of our friendship. If someone had drama, it was all our drama.

So when I came on *TOWIE* and the girls had their drama with the other girls, my instant reaction was to back them up, but when shit hit the fan for me, they just weren't up for fighting my battles too. Looking back, I think Chloe and Courtney constantly wanted to fit in better with the others, even if that meant losing their best friend. The whole episode really opened my eyes.

So within a couple of months of joining the show, I felt pretty isolated. I had Pete, but every girl needs her girlfriends. Unfortunately, mine were more worried about fitting in with the rest of the cast, when really what should have mattered was our twenty-year friendship and what that had meant to us during all those years. Instead, it was clear some people wanted me gone, not just from the lunch hall, but from *TOWIE* completely.

From then on, I have to say, the fun times I had on *TOWIE* were pretty limited. Every day just got really hard with all the agg and tension between everyone. Chloe admitted it was hard to be friends with the other girls as well as me, and I used to say to her, 'I've been your friend for twenty years. They're using you to get to me.' But she didn't want to hear it – she felt pulled between us, between me and those girls who'd known her five minutes.

I tried to sort it out with Chloe behind the scenes, either phoning or texting her – not going to lie, I did send her some harsh messages, but that's coming from someone really hurt about losing their best friend since childhood – but what I kept finding was that, if I messaged her about something, she'd tell the producers, and, the next thing I knew, it was another storyline on the show. I wanted to keep some important stuff away from it, but it seemed like Girl Band had other ideas, and the producers obviously didn't mind – for them, the more personal it was, the better. We had a long, real-life friendship to mend, but I knew that was never going to happen on camera.

Things came to a head during what would turn out to be one of our very last big scenes together. I'd just moved into my new flat, and all my real-life besties had been talking about coming round to see it and bringing me a housewarming present. On the day of my move, Amber turned up, Maddie turned up, but there was no sign of Chloe and this obviously upset me.

We arranged to meet, in a field, as you do, and it was all caught on camera for *TOWIE*. I tried to explain how I felt. I told her, 'I feel a bit distant. I've always had your back and you haven't had mine.'

She said straight away, 'You didn't even invite me to your house,' but that made me cross, and I forgot all about the cameras. I told her, 'Don't bullshit me, I know there was a group chat, I know you knew when I was moving. You don't need a phone call to turn up. You're my best mate.' That was true – we hadn't phoned each other to arrange a meeting for years. We both knew that was rubbish. It was obviously an excuse. I felt she was making a big thing out of this, but it was pretty intense and upsetting, all the same.

So the longest friendship of my life ended in a field, with the cameras rolling. We screamed at each other, we both cried and it was terrible. We didn't speak for a year after that – that's right, a WHOLE YEAR. We literally used to walk past each other without making eye contact. If we were made to work together, we'd sit in the same room without looking at each other. It was possibly one of the hardest things I've had to do.

I decided to be civil, even though I'd already decided I wouldn't talk to her again. I was on the show for a year-and- a-half, and this state of affairs lasted almost the whole final year of that. We got through it somehow.

I know we were both really hurt. We'd gone through all those years together, making our way to and from stage school, dreaming our big dreams. Our families knew each other, our lives had always been shared, and now that we were actually living the dream, we should have been enjoying it together. Instead, here we were, ignoring each other. It was just really, really sad.

The one chance Chloe had to win my friendship back came a while later, when we all flew to Marbella. I was going through an absolute nightmare with Pete by then

– she knew about it and texted me once we got to the hotel, saying, 'I'm here if you need to talk,' which I thought was genuine.

But she didn't say anything else, and she didn't come to see me when I was sitting in my room crying. It ended up being Danielle Armstrong who came to check on me, even though before that, I wouldn't have called her a close friend. Chloe never showed up, and instead, the next day, she showed others the text she'd sent me saying, 'She didn't reply.' Once again, our private messages were being shown to others. By then, it didn't even surprise me.

By the time I decided to leave the show, we'd somehow found a way of speaking civilly to each other when we needed to. They put me and Chloe together for one final scene, and someone said, 'Maybe we can get Girl Band back on track.' I replied, 'No. Girl Band's dead.'

My restaurant, the McK Grill in Woodford, launched in May 2017 – everyone was invited from *TOWIE*, but Chloe made a big deal on camera about not coming. For me, that's when I knew I was done.

That same month, Dan Edgar had a birthday party for the series finale, and we all found ourselves in the same spot. Chloe told me she missed me and our long friendship, but I felt like I had to spell it all out again for her. Just because you keep saying you're sad about something, doesn't mean it's suddenly okay. Yes, she'd been my mate for twenty years, but she'd also let me down. I think we both still wanted to rescue it, but it just didn't happen.

Since leaving the show, she and I have had very little communication – just the odd text, low-level stuff. Recently, she messaged me to say happy birthday, and I'll send her something similar, so it's just a civil thing like that. To me, she chose *TOWIE* over our friendship, but for me twenty years of memories are hard to forget and it still leaves me feeling sad. But life goes on. We still live in the same Essex bubble and we're always going to bump into each other. I'm pleased we can smile now and say hello when we do.

Looking back on *TOWIE* from where I'm sitting now, I can safely say it's one of the hardest things I've ever done, much harder than the previous shows I went on, even harder than *CBB*. I became such a big part of the storyline in such a short time, that other people knew if they attached something to me, it would work for them, too. That made it almost impossible for me to escape, and meant I was always surrounded by a lot of drama, even the stuff I didn't bring on myself.

But you know what? It made for some great TV and brought me some amazing opportunities. Plus, looking back, they were all just moments in time that could have happened to anyone – my ones just happened to get caught on camera. The real challenge for me in the future is not being known as 'Megan McKenna from *TOWIE*', but just 'Megan McKenna'.

21

'Are you fucking joking me?' I probably said that phrase about a thousand times while I was on *TOWIE*. Pretty much as soon as I became part of that whole world, I had friendships breaking down, loads of rival cliques forming and me shouting and crying all over the place. I can honestly say, though, all the way through, me and Pete... we were as thick as thieves pretty much the whole first two series I was on there. It was only when the texting thing happened that things went downhill fast... but we'll get to that.

Don't forget, things were all pretty new between me and him anyway, but then we had all them challenges that every couple faces on reality TV, where people just can't help themselves but stir the pot. It was clear back then that Pete completely had my back. By the end of the first series, we were falling for each other. Then, just in time for the final episode, we made things official.

At the beginning of the next series, we were all out in Marbella and there were rubbish stories about me – apparently the breaking news was that I'd been spotted 'all over someone' at a party. People were telling me, 'We have pictures to prove it.' I knew it was bollocks, so I just said, 'Show me the pictures,' and they backed off. But these rumours did cause a bit of a stir between me and Pete, and I felt a bit bad even though I'd done nothing, because he seemed a bit cut up by it all. Later, I just thought what a cheek he had to play along and act like the victim, making me feel so guilty, even though that Marbella thing was so ridiculous. But at the time I just thought it must be horrible to hear.

Then he told me on camera, 'At the end of the day, no one is going to come between me and you as far as I'm concerned. I'm always going to have your back. I trust you one hundred per cent and we're a team.

'I stuck around because I believed in you, and it's made me realise I've fallen in love with you, and that I'm glad that I met you, and that you've become part of my life.'

Well, what girl wouldn't like to hear that? I really need to learn not to trust these Essex boys. And it makes my blood boil now to remember all that shit he came out with. He was so happy to play the victim, the understanding boyfriend. At the time, I felt sorry for him. Later, when it all came to light, I found out he wasn't exactly being an angel himself back then.

When we first started dating, it was pretty casual, but you'd be amazed how *TOWIE* can speed everything up. It's impossible to have a normal relationship. Either you're talking about your feelings for each other, or everyone else is weighing in with their opinion of the situation. After two whole dates, it becomes, 'Are you official now?' You never really have the option to be 'seeing someone' for a while and just hanging out with each other. I wouldn't say it forced our relationship into anything it wouldn't have been anyway – I did like him, plus back then, he liked to party, and what girl doesn't like to party? – but it was definitely rushed.

The whole story might get played out more gradually, but apart from that, it's just like *Ex on the Beach*. Everything is heightened, and my relationship with Pete was definitely pushed forward by months. We'd have had all those months to get to know each other properly, but that wasn't how it panned out.

I had some lovely times with Pete Wicks. We went to some really nice places – twice on holiday to Dubai, and also Miami and Vegas. These were private holidays, not a TV camera in sight, and we had loads of fun messing about, being silly and being proper boyfriend and girlfriend. What he did to me later was appalling, there's no getting away from it, but I can't slate him for those early months. He was a real gentleman and treated me like a princess.

In September 2016, just before we were due to start filming another series, Pete and I went on holiday to Barcelona. I thought everything was really good between us, and that was the trip where we took that picture of us in our hotel bathroom that went viral. Both of us were in our birthday suits – me completely naked, but somehow covering my naughty bits with the edge of the bath, and Pete stood behind me wearing only his tattoos. God, how cringe! The boys on *TOWIE* took the mick out of us for ages.

So there were still some good times, but I was also starting to get a BAD VIBE. You know that feeling, right? Pete just seemed to be off with me – all distracted, a bit snappy. And his behaviour was making me paranoid, so I probably wasn't as much fun as I used to be. A few weeks before, my family had all got together at my parents' house to celebrate my granddad's birthday. Everybody liked Pete, so he'd naturally been invited, but he was very distant while he was there. Now here we were on holiday together, and the atmosphere was, well, let's just put it this way... it was fucking shit.

The next thing I knew, there were all these stories in the press – me and Pete, both on our phones, not looking at each other, not talking, and the headlines were all about us 'running out of conversation'. I was just really confused, although to be honest, they got it right – we weren't really talking.

There was already loads of tension between us, and this just made things worse. I was getting more and more paranoid and I was crying every night, worrying that it was all going wrong. Then, right in the middle of the holiday, we had to fly back to London, for the TV Choice Awards. They say the camera never lies – well, that's a lie. Them pictures of us on the red carpet showed us all tanned and smiley, looking like the perfect, happy couple – but I can remember thinking that night, 'I'm not sure I even want to fly back to Barcelona.' That's how bad things were.

I still had no idea what was really going on. The penny didn't drop for another couple of weeks, when it was a couple of days before my birthday.

We were at my flat together, and Pete fell asleep with his arm across me on the sofa. By now, I'd had a bad feeling for weeks. I promise you I'd not once been through his phone before, but it was time. Whatever was going on, I felt like I needed to know. I felt a bit sick, but it had to happen. I thought I was going mad.

Firstly, can I just say that I could be a professional private investigator? Do you know how I got his password? I remembered the code he'd told me for the safe in the hotel room, and I wondered if that was his phone code too.

So I tried it, and... ping, it unlocked. I mean, come on now, how stupid can you be? I'm not as thick as people think. I went through everything, and – guess what – nothing! No texts, no WhatsApp messages, nothing at all. So then I checked his Instagram and Twitter, and there were some messages from girls, plus some replies from him. Bastard! I quickly took some screen grabs to send to my phone, so I could show him when he woke up. (Another thing a girl needs to do: KEEP THE EVIDENCE.)

Then I sat there for a while. Those messages I'd found were pretty rude, but they weren't enough to explain his bad mood with me, his lack of interest, all that shit between us. I thought, 'There has to be something else.' I thought, 'There's more.' I just had a feeling in my belly.

Pete stayed asleep and his arm was still round me, so I picked up his phone again and looked for the archived messages folder. I clicked on it, and there they all were – at least ten different girls.

I felt paralysed. I had that sinking feeling – I'm sure everyone can relate to that feeling. I knew then that nothing between us was going to be the same again.

I tried to click through all the messages quickly. I was screen grabbing some of them and sending them to my phone. I noticed he was messaging one of the girls more than the others. She looked nothing like me. WTF? I wrote her name in my phone and sent myself more and more screen grabs. Honestly, I reckon

I could have worked for MI5, I was that quick! Then I started calculating the dates, and I realised loads of the messages were six months old, but they went all the way up to this exact night.

The thing that really got to me? I realised one of the dates when he'd been chatting to that particular girl was the same day he'd been with my family for my late granddad's celebration. There's my family all together, crying and laughing. And there's Pete, supposedly one of my family, asking this girl about her holiday. She was telling him she had freckles and was wearing a bikini, and he was answering, 'I love freckles.' With a heart-eye emoji. I was literally thinking, 'WTF – he's speaking to her exactly the way he speaks to me.' The messages to this girl went back over the last six months. I was GUTTED!

After a while, I'd had enough, so I shut his phone down, waited for a while and then woke him up. I don't know how I sat there but I did, and Pete woke up to the sound of me reading aloud all these little conversations. At first, he was confused, and asked, 'What are you doing?' Then, when he realised what was going on, he shouted, 'Why are you going down my phone?' The sound of a guilty man. Well, that set me off.

I was screaming at him – like you would – but for some reason I kept bringing up the past as well.

'I've had this done to me before, and now you've done it. How dare you?'

A lot of this hurt was about Pete, but a lot of it was definitely about The Dip and how he'd treated me all those years before. This just showed I'd never really got over that. For me, it all felt like fresh salt on the wound again.

Pete finally left, and I went through all the messages again. There was plenty of X-rated stuff, but the one that hurt me the most wasn't even that rude. One girl sent him a picture of herself – I could see her legs in a pair of knickers in front of the telly with a big close-up face on the screen. And it was my face! Really! Now, I'm sorry, but that's pretty dark. That's what she'd been sending him, and although he hadn't entertained that picture, he'd still continued to message her. That's what made me lose it. I was fuming. I don't even know if they ever met up – he always said they didn't and that he never physically cheated, but for me that picture was bad enough, and it made me lose my shit all over again.

I followed Pete to his car, pulled the cigarette out of his mouth and grabbed him. I was holding him by the arm, saying, 'You have fucking ruined me.' It was four o'clock in the morning and I was completely sober – this wasn't like a Nu Bar tantrum – but I went completely fucking mental. He kept telling me to calm down, but he knew he'd done this to me, so he took it. I was screaming at him, 'You have fucking broken my heart again.' I kept saying, 'Again and again.'

It wasn't a good look. Pete stayed in his car; I went back inside my flat and eventually began to calm down a bit. My mum turned up really early in the morning and we had a cup of tea together. She couldn't believe it either. Like I said, everyone in my family liked Pete a lot. They were all as stunned as me by this other side of him. When he was with us, he always held himself like this old-fashioned gentleman. He'd made me feel like a princess the whole time I was with him, and now it turned out there was this other side that I didn't know anything about. It was genuinely like he was two different people. How could he lie next to me, tell me he loved me, say that I was the best girl he ever had, while doing all this? I just couldn't make any sense of it; it felt like I didn't know him at all.

Eventually, I went out to the car to talk to him. I made him ring one of the girls and tell her he couldn't speak to her any more. I think this was me trying to get some control over a situation where it felt like I'd had it all taken away from me. At one point, I saw red again. I grabbed the phone from him while he was talking to her and shouted at her myself, warning her, 'Don't you ever come near me.' She couldn't believe it was me on the phone. Then I deleted all the numbers in his phone. I think he thought that was a step towards me forgiving him, but straight after, I told him we were done.

The timing could not have been worse. We were all due to fly to Marbella to film the next series of

TOWIE. I told Pete, 'You've made life so difficult for me now.'

I left him there in the car, and I didn't speak to him for a few days. That was when he started to seriously grovel. When I say begging, I mean BEGGING! He sent me flowers, he turned up at my door, he turned up at my parents' door, but none of us could handle seeing him. Meanwhile, no one had any idea what was going on, and, all of a sudden, it was time to fly off to Marbella. Happy families, everyone.

I had no idea what to do, if I'm honest. I was absolutely gutted about the whole thing, but Pete sat me down and said enough good stuff to make me think he'd learnt his lesson and wouldn't be doing any of it again.

He told me he would never do this again, that he was going to change, and that it had made him realise how much he did love me. Like I said, he fed me some good lines, and with *TOWIE* waiting for us to confirm our flights to Spain to film together, I had a decision to make.

By this point, a big part of what I felt was actually relief – turned out all that paranoia I'd been feeling for so many weeks was justified, and I wasn't actually going mad – so that was a positive. I also thought he deserved a second chance, because there were loads of genuinely good things between us.

So, yeah, I did decide to forgive him and take him back. Plus, I promised I wouldn't tell anybody about these texts I'd found – which I thought was a pretty massive gesture, considering all the shit he'd put me through. But he'd been one of the only people looking out for me on the show, and it felt only right to give him a chance to make it up to me.

So I faked my best smile and it was off to Marbella.

By the time we got to Marbella, I'm not going to lie, I had a bit of hate for him. I was finding it pretty difficult to just pretend nothing had happened. Pete and I had a couple of rows about it, and the rest of the cast started to notice that something was up, but boys being boys, they decided to blame me for it instead of him.

Pete's mate Lockie said on camera, 'Megan never lets Pete come out any more.' What they didn't realise was that I was still hurting, trying to learn to trust him again. No one knew what was behind my change of mood; instead, they just made stupid jokes about me trying to control him.

One day, we were at a pool party, and a girl came over to Pete to talk to him. By now, I was so paranoid that I kept looking across while he had his picture taken with her. Then she carried on trying to get his attention, and I went a bit mad. Everyone was saying, 'Megan needs to take a chill pill, it's just a fan.' Meanwhile, I'd burst into tears. We had to go and film our loved-up opening credits and from the outside, we looked like the perfect power couple. In reality, we weren't even talking. But I still didn't tell the producers there was a problem.

The first episode of the new series actually made me laugh out loud – there's Pete giving his mate Lockie all this mature, wise advice about relationships. There's Pete telling him, 'Sometimes, even if you love something, you have to walk away if it ain't right.' He said, 'The worst thing you can do is try and do something you ain't ready to do.' Ha ha. How ironic is that?

We did our best to patch things up. The next day was the day before my birthday, and Pete appeared with flowers, a card, a present, everything a girl could want. He sat down with me and read the card out, which must have been a bit weird for everyone who didn't know we had any problems. I'd stuck to my promise of not mentioning anything, so they must have been wondering what was going on when Pete started reading what he'd written.

He said, 'Megan, this may be your first birthday with me, but it won't be your last. I have my faults, and you've stood by me, and I thank you for that. I've so much admiration for you and everything you've achieved, and

I'm lucky to have you in my life. I'm behind you no matter what. You're my best friend and the best girlfriend a geezer could ask for, and I love you.'

He'd got me a very nice present as well – viewers watched him hand over this Rolex, which he spent a fortune on, and yeah, I was over the moon. But people give me shit on social media about 'still wearing Pete's watch', so now let me set the record straight. Yes I do wear a beautiful watch, but it's not the one that Pete bought me, it's a new one. Also, what people need to know is that I spoiled him too. We were both very generous – isn't that what you do in relationships? – and me and him both realise that a present is a present, and neither of us has ever asked for anything back. So yeah, I do wear a beautiful watch. I've worked my arse off to buy myself nice things, and also treat the people I love, and I certainly don't need anyone else to buy them for me.

I was still very happy that day, and I shared a picture on Instagram, where I thanked him for my lovely present. I wrote on Twitter, 'Omggggggggggg legit the most spoilt girl ever,' while he wrote, 'Happy birthday to my best friend, girlfriend and the bird that makes me a better geezer.'

This little display of public affection is probably what stirred up a certain lady back in the UK, and that's when the papers possibly got another telephone call. Stand by for some fireworks in Marbella...

There I was, with Danielle. I'd confided in her that I was worried because Pete was always off with me, and she was really sympathetic. Then I noticed Pete himself was walking around the side of the pool where Danni and I were sitting. I thought that was pretty weird – other people don't normally appear like that when you're filming.

Next thing I knew, Danni had to leave. At this moment in time, my IBS was playing up, and I felt like I was going to get the shits. I was getting a weird vibe, so I made someone tell me what was going on. Then Danni came back, and she looked as though she'd seen a ghost. She said to me, 'I feel awkward, but I've seen something about Pete texting a girl.' I thought she must mean 'the girl in the picture' all over again, but Danni said it was somebody with brown hair. She didn't know a lot about it, but what she did say was tough enough to hear – stuff like the girl saying, 'I wish you were single,' and Pete replying, 'Tell me about it,' and 'I can't wait to get home.' What a wanker!

I had that same sinking feeling in my belly all over again, but I tried to keep calm, and I said, 'I've found some messages, but I'm not sure. I need to find out what I'm talking about.'

So I made the producers tell me what was going on – I went off camera, and someone finally gave me a phone to read all the stuff online. It was an exclusive in the *Sun*, and they didn't hold back. The article was an interview with a girl called Jacqui, an ex of Pete's, and she told them he'd been messaging her the whole time we were in Barcelona.

Turned out the papers had got it both right and wrong. We WERE both on our phones, but one of us definitely hadn't run out of conversation, judging by them texts.

He'd been telling her how boring I was, that I hardly drank, that he couldn't wait to get home, that he missed being single. Some of their messages were X-rated, and the *Sun* said some of them were too rude to print. Trust me, it was brutal. Who wants to read about their boyfriend talking about anal sex?!

What made me really mad, though, was the angle this girl took in the interview. She went on and on about 'what a dog' Pete was, how sorry she felt for me, and that if she was me, she'd be really hurt. But she was the one going along with him, and she was the one giving them the story! It was beyond humiliating.

I couldn't believe what I was reading. I finished the article and went back on camera, and then Pete turned up. Danni gave him a dirty look, and then she was gone and it was just me and him. Everything you can see in that scene was 100 per cent real – I had found out literally only minutes before, and I was beside myself. I thought I had no words but, as you saw, I somehow found them. I walked away and went so crazy.

Another thing that got me raging was remembering my promise not to bring anything up about the previous messages. The cameras were rolling and I went at him, 'I wasn't going to say anything, was I? Now I'm mortified.'

Pete said, 'I haven't been near a bird. I fucked up.' He kept saying they were the same messages, like he was trying to make out it was an old crime, and there was nothing new to worry about. What he didn't realise was that it wasn't even the content of the messages themselves, though that was bad enough. My problem was, he'd known they were out there and that they could come back to shoot us both in the arse, but instead he'd just put his trust in these girls not to say anything.

I spotted the Rolex on my wrist, and that only set me off again. 'That's guilt, that is,' I shouted, waving it around. I'd found it weird in the first place that he'd wanted to get me that amazing present. Now I knew why.

Eventually, I screamed, 'You're telling a girl you want to be single. Fucking go and be single.'

I walked off and went so crazy that security had to pull me away. We were kept in separate rooms for the rest of the day, although at some point I managed to escape and started kicking down his hotel room door. It was all getting a bit too much, so they arranged to send Pete home on his own.

The next thing I knew, his management decided to release a statement without my permission, saying, basically, that I knew all about the messages and that me and Pete were getting through it. Hang on a minute!

Yes, I knew about some of them, but not all of them, and not that he'd been lying next to me, telling some other girl he wanted to do rude things to her. I was raging with him, and equally pissed off at her. She used this whole situation to get herself some headlines, and even called herself a 'girl's girl', so I asked her on social media why she didn't message me herself. No reply. Well, what could she say?

I went out that night, got absolutely smashed, paralytic, went home and did a tell-all video on Snapchat. I was pissed and crying, with my mascara running down my cheeks. I looked a state, but I could still speak.

In the video I said, 'I did know about some messages that were going about and obviously that's hurt a lot.

'That a boy I thought loved me and I loved could be with me and doing that at the same time.

'But then, like, today, for some girl to sell a story about it, and for me to see the messages that I hadn't seen before – that fucking hurts.

'She's obviously seen that me and him were trying to move on, and obviously he's bought me nice things, and I put it on Instagram and Twitter, and it's rubbed her up the wrong way.

'But just to clear those rumours up – I didn't know all those messages were going about, but it's fucking hurtful and heartbreaking. I just wish none of this had happened really.'

183

Then I signed off: 'Life's a c**t. Everything happens for a reason.'

Beautiful words.

In the end I just bunged it on Snapchat, because I didn't want anyone twisting my words. The next day, what I'd said got reported in every paper. I think I made my point.

My tips for the perfect girls' night out

💋 Start with Porn Star Martinis at home

💋 Get ready with everyone together

💋 Get yourself a good camera with a timer (Amber was always an expert at getting the best angle in group selfies)

💋 Be honest – if your mate looks like a mess, tell her. Help the girl out before you get out the door!

💋 Bring nail glue. You never know what's going to break #toenailgate

💋 Always end the night out on a Maccy D's (if anyone wants to know my actual order, it's a double cheeseburger, extra pickles, no bun, large fries and a Fanta)

💋 The perfect hangover cure: Spaghetti Bolognese for breakfast and Capri Suns

23

It feels like girls losing their rag have always been given a bad time for it. Danni put her finger on it in Marbella. She said, 'Blokes treat us like this, then they blame us when we go psycho.' I thought, 'She's absolutely nailed it,' and I do always wonder what that's all about. It's just one more reason why us girls have to stick together.

What's the most annoying thing in this world? Being lied to and told you're just paranoid when you ask if something's wrong. Okay, so what's the second most annoying? I'd say it's when somebody finally confesses, but then refuses to explain themselves. And that's what happened between me and Pete after our return to Essex.

For one of my first scenes back home, I was sitting in my flat with my sister when he appeared. It was the first time we'd spoken in ages, but there was no way of mending it because he wouldn't explain why he'd done what he did. He just said, 'I can't give you a reason, because I don't have one. If I could answer, it'd be easier.'

He did look pretty sad, but I can't begin to explain how frustrating it is being told, 'I can't give you a reason,' after someone's treated you that badly. Eventually, he said, 'I fucked up because I never thought I deserved you in the first place.' Hmm. What a load of bollocks.

I told him, 'The worst thing is, you know I've been through this all before. You've embarrassed me.'

And that was a massive part of it, to be honest. On the one hand, it was hard being lied to, definitely. But I reckon I actually could have coped with that, if we'd been able to sit down and work it out. After all, like he said, 'I never cheated on you.'

No, the real problem for me was the public humiliation of it – all them people watching *TOWIE*, all our followers on social media, everyone reading the papers – I just couldn't bear it. I know people would say that's the price of having a public profile, but at that point, it felt like the cost was far too high.

Meanwhile, Pete was still grovelling, telling me on screen, 'I don't expect you to get back with me now, but you need to know I love you, and I won't give up, because I know you still love me.'

I have to say he worked hard, that boy. He went and said sorry to my sister, my mum and my dad. He even got a tattoo on his hand with my initial. We went on a spa date – obviously the cameras were there – where there was wine and flowers. He told me, 'I'm not going to give up. This is going to affect the rest of my life.'

Pete really did pull out all the stops. He knew my favourite soppy tune was 'Endless Love' by Lionel Richie and Diana Ross, so guess what was playing on the PA system when we sat down to dinner at the hotel? He'd arranged the whole thing. It was pretty cute. But what's annoying now is, he's ruined that fucking song for me. Then, for his birthday, I gave him a Louis Vuitton luggage set and a memory book which took me days to make, all about us. He read the card, and had a little cry. And we had our first proper kiss since the whole nightmare began.

Love's young dream, back on track? Well, yes and no. Yes, it was all great again between us – he'd swept me off my feet. But, despite all my pleading with him to explain, Pete had never been able to come up with any actual reason for his behaviour. He could never tell me why it all happened, which is why I don't think we ever properly resolved it. And I stayed pretty uneasy about the whole thing.

On the surface, it was a case of new era, new rules, but he kept slipping up. I knew he had a contract with Ann Summers, and I always said, 'Do what you got to do, it's work,' but of course I was still a bit paranoid. Then, off he went for a shoot one day, and he said, 'Nothing too explicit. Just promoting underwear.' Later on, he showed me some of the shots, and he was right, there was nothing too bad going on. He looked nice. Proud girlfriend.

Which was all fine until... We were due to film *Celebrity Juice* together one evening, but in the morning I woke up to a tweet from one of the magazines, saying, 'Sure Megan won't be happy with this.' So of course, I clicked on the link. It was the same shoot he'd told me about, but – what a surprise – the pictures weren't the ones I'd already seen. In one of them, one of the girls in lingerie even has a whip placed on Pete's bare chest! So I lost my shit all over again. And then – with our usual shit timing – we had to go and film a scene for *TOWIE* together.

It was in a really nice restaurant, and my parents had put on a birthday lunch for him, but he turned up all shame-faced, telling them, 'We've had a barney again.'

That scene was so bad. If you watch it now, you can see that I had hardly any makeup on, because I'd been in my flat having a complete breakdown just before filming. I had the producers calling me, and I was beside myself, hysterical, not knowing what to do. The texting thing was out in the press, and I was back with him, but it was all a massive struggle and I felt really insecure, really fragile. All I wanted was honesty and respect, but it felt like he just couldn't give that to me.

And now here is, Pirate Pete, at his most polite and charming. 'I knew you'd laid this on, so I didn't want to let you down,' he told my parents. 'I didn't want to ruin your lunch. Thank you for this.' His little humble act made me sick. I was fuming, and even my dad – never the one to speak out, always prefers to keep his opinions to himself – he actually said something this time. 'It's a bit embarrassing, isn't it?' Coming from my dad, that meant a lot.

I definitely did over-react on this occasion. I screamed at Pete, 'You're a fucking liar, you lie to me all the time.' He stormed off, and my parents just sat there, saying nothing. Eventually, my mum said that I either had to forgive him and move on, or forget him. Fair point, I suppose. Pete said the same thing, saying he was always worried about pissing me off, even while I was asking him to be more open with me. It was becoming harder and harder to respect each other, though, particularly when other people kept putting their oar in, some innocently, some not so much.

That very same night, the pair of us had to paste our best smiles back on and go and film *Celebrity Juice*. We sat in complete silence in the car on the way there, but it was so bad once we got there, we had to have separate dressing rooms. This should have been a real high point in both our careers – one of the best TV shows you can get in the reality game. Instead, it just became more and more awkward as Keith Lemon asked us stuff like, 'Who would you have in a threesome?' You have to be professional, and somehow I managed to keep the smile on my face even when Pete made a few digs at me – at one point he called me his 'ex-girlfriend' – and Keith made some digs about the texting. On the recording, you can see me laughing away. Honestly, I should have got an Oscar that night! Inside I was fuming.

It seemed as if all the trust and respect that had been there at the beginning of our relationship had disappeared. I started getting abuse on social media – people were asking me, 'Where is your self-respect? I wonder if you gave your other exes a third chance,' or telling me, 'If Pete truly loved you he wouldn't be messaging other girls... simple.' Someone asked me, 'Silly girl, he will only do the same thing again and again! Why would you give that cheat a third time?'

Good question! What can I tell you to explain it? I can only say that, at the time, after all the drama we'd been through together, being without him would have felt a bit... weird. On a personal level, it was like we'd become used to that level of agg in our relationship. I know that sounds really bad, but I have to be honest! And, don't forget, he did keep telling me he really did love me. Besides, that person on social media was right – I HAD given my other exes third chances and more, so I clearly needed to work on my self-esteem a bit.

24

It was March 2017 and it seemed to everyone that it
was all smooth sailing between Pete and me. Pete was
telling people how we'd finally got this whole relationship
business sussed. He said to them, 'We're getting on really
well. It's taken time, but now we get it. You know what
pushes each other's buttons, and you realise that, and you
stop pushing them.'

Well, all I can say is, if I'd been downing my glass
of wine, it would have been spat at the screen. In the
weeks leading up to that grand speech, Pete and I must
have gone through the whole break-up-make-up routine
about half a dozen times. It was always the same —
some tiny thing causing a massive row, one of us driving
off in the car, the other one deleting all our pictures

from social media, then someone (okay, that'll be me) driving round to his house and shouting 'Let me in!' like a psycho.

Pete was probably being a bit more accurate when he said, 'She's really vocal about how she feels. I ain't, but I've got to let her in more. We've got to work on the communication more, because I'm shit at it.'

The truth of the matter was, we weren't making each other happy, but neither of us was prepared to say it out loud. Simple as that. For our one-year anniversary, we went away to a hotel with the film crew. There were scones, strawberries, champagne on ice – the full romantic works. But I couldn't sit there and fake my feelings any longer.

When he asked, 'Who'd have thought we'd make a year?' even Pete didn't sound convinced. I tried to tell him how his constant bad mood was affecting me, but he just said it was the same for him. It wasn't like our other big rows – this chat was actually more sad than angry. I cried, and that's when he told me, 'I'd take six bad days for the one day that we are good.'

With his next breath, though, he was moaning, 'I've wasted a year of my fucking life,' and he stormed off.

We were meant to stay the night, but he left and I had to drive home with one of the producers. As I was packing up, I noticed Pete had left that memory book I gave him, and he'd finished the pages... A few months later, I burned that same book, took a video and sent it to him. Yes, pretty psycho I know.

The thing is, that's all fine when you're a teenager and you don't mind being a bit dramatic – and I should know, Nu Bar anyone? – but nobody should have to go through six shitty days with anybody for one good day, and I think we both realised that. Pete was clearly miserable – I couldn't make him happy and I couldn't trust him after everything we'd gone through.

A few days after that, we sat down together in my flat, and I really think he thought we were going to give it another go. Instead, I told him the truth: 'I wanted it to work. I just can't deal with it. It's not fair on you that I can't forgive you.'

Pete asked, 'Why can't you forgive me?' OMG! I don't know what it is, but this just used to frustrate me. I must have told him a million times, but now I told him again – it was because he'd never actually explained his bad behaviour to me, so how could I learn to deal with it?

He lost his temper and shouted, 'Because I can't explain it! What happened was shit, and I can't feel guilty about it all the time. I can't pay for that for the rest of my life.'

It slowly dawned on him that this wasn't going well. 'Is that it then? Are we just going to call it a day? Are you still in love with me?'

I took a deep breath. 'I feel like I love you but I feel different. I feel like you've pushed me away.'

That was me saying, but in a pretty wimp way, that I felt like there was no love there – he'd just pushed me too far.

All this shit was going on, but when it came on TV and I watched it back, all I could see was my bloody eyelash stuck to my eyebrow. How embarrassing, ha ha. And people say *TOWIE*'s fake! That was it – we'd broken up. I was single.

In the days afterwards, there were a few messages back and forth, but as far as I was concerned, we were finally in the past. At this point, I needed a change of scene, so I took up an invitation for a night out at an Essex club.

It was indeed the very same club where I'd gone with The Dip all those years before. God, why out of all places, did I decide to go there? #prat. So much time had passed – I had no idea if he was going to be there, I just knew I'd had enough of sitting in feeling sorry for myself, and it was time to catch up with some old friends and make some new ones. So off I went, hair all blow-dried, wearing a silk mini-dress, and I did have lots of fun. I bumped into The Dip's mates and we had a right laugh. I was just saying to them, 'I haven't been here since you know who,' when a very familiar face appeared in front of me – Mr Dip himself.

I went to the bar, and there he was. 'All right, Meg?' 'All right.' I didn't speak to him properly until the end of the night. We ended up having a chat when the lights had come up, and I started getting a bit emotional. He asked me, 'Are you back with Pete?' and I told him we'd broken up. Then it was time for me to go home. I got in a taxi with Amber and just burst into tears. What a state! At this point, Amber looked at me and said, 'Are you really crying over Pete or The Dip?' I said, 'I just don't know.'

After the weekend, me and Pete spoke a bit – still on bad terms – but then had another huge argument, and we were back on that break again. I thought, 'Fuck this, I'm going out again,' so I went to Sheesh in Chigwell. And guess what? There he was – The Dip staring straight at me! Can you believe it? I promise you I hadn't seen him in two full years, and now here we were, in the same place twice in the same week. That night we sat chatting – we talked all about the past, and eventually I kissed him.

Yep, I know. Quite dramatic. But to be honest, whatever might have been going on in my own head, I really didn't think I had any explaining to do. Everyone knew I was single once more – God knows, they'd heard enough about the Megan and Pete rollercoaster – but everyone, and I mean EVERYONE, pretty much ran over to Team Pete without even talking to me about it. Inevitably, there were all sorts of rumours going round that I'd cheated on Pete with my ex. I had to use every chance I could get to explain myself, which made for some pretty awkward moments.

'How I deal with things is I go out and get smashed,' I said. 'I went out, my ex was there, we had a few drinks. I've done nothing wrong – I'm completely single, I can do what I want. What I don't want is these rumours being blown out of proportion.' As if that would happen!

Look, I know this all makes me look like a twat, but I was an emotional wreck, and I think Pete realised that, which was why he decided to get over the whole drama with The Dip. Not saying it was right. Yes, it was too soon. But I just wasn't in the right frame of mind.

Despite splitting up and having all this mature chat, Pete and I still managed to steal the show with an almighty blow-up halfway through the series – a scene that went viral, became one of *TOWIE*'s biggest ever fights between any couple, and inspired about a million memes.

We were stood in the street. It all started off quite calmly, with me telling him I was a bit upset about some things the others had been saying, and asking him to stop other people getting involved in all our stuff. Then, I did this big sigh, basically because I was so fucked off with him always playing the good guy – and I said so.

Next thing I knew, he was screaming at me, 'So you was an angel? I never went near another fucking bird.' And off he went again about how I'd never forgiven him, how he'd tried everything, and how it could have worked. What planet was he on? It was just bollocks. It was like he'd forgotten how fucking miserable he was the entire time –

he was making up this entire story in his head. It made me livid all over again. I screamed at him, 'It's a load of shit. I don't believe it.' I started walking away and he followed me, but I'd had enough. I told him, 'You're fake,' and that was it. The only thing good about that scene was how amazing my hair looked, LOL.

Somehow, even after that, we managed to calm down and agree not to listen to anyone else weighing in on our relationship. For a while, it seemed as though we might actually be friends.

Don't hold your breath, guys! By the following month, we were being very friendly to each other. For the series finale, we were all at a pool party for Dan Edgar's birthday, and Pete and I were flirting across the pool. I know, I know! But somehow, despite all the bollocks we'd put each other through, another romantic reunion was on the cards. In fact nobody knew, but we stayed in the same hotel room that night – just in time for me to head off to Nashville.

This time, we decided to be all grown up, make it official, not put everything on camera, enjoy our time together in the break from filming and give it one last shot. Off I went to America, and things were sweet.

25

'What are your own goals?' my therapist asked me.

'Leave all this negativity behind and follow your own path,' my mum reminded me.

Well, that's all a bit easier said than done when you're in the middle of your own massive reality TV psychodrama! All it had been was meltdowns and mayhem. Every single day was agg. But somehow, despite all that, I never completely let go of my biggest dreams – you remember the ones I told you all about?... Writing songs, recording tracks, going out on the road and, most importantly of all, getting on that tour bus!

All my life, I'd belted out a song whenever I got the chance. When I was little, it was my parents, nan and granddad who were my audience. Even back then, I took it all very seriously, having mini-meltdowns if it didn't go properly and having little hissy fits if I didn't get my song just right.

My voice had caught some people by surprise along the way. I'd had that sing-off in *Ex on the Beach*, and I'd had to sing for one of the tasks during *Celebrity Big Brother*. I remember one of the best things about that whole experience was being able to surprise people. The look on Darren Day's face when I opened my mouth and he realised I could actually hold a tune! To be fair to them, after all my screaming, a ballad wasn't exactly what they were expecting. But it's all part of me. I'm definitely as musical as I am mouthy.

More recently, I got a fresh taste for singing when I got the chance to perform live on the West End stage just before Christmas 2016. Two of *Strictly*'s best ever dancers, Gleb Savchenko and Kristina Rihanoff, were in a show called *One More Dance* at the Adelphi Theatre on the Strand. As well as them dancing, the show also had singers from the West End, including a girl called Louise Dearman. She'd played Elphaba and Glinda in the West End production of *Wicked*, which just happens to be my favourite ever musical. So it was pretty overwhelming for me to be sharing the stage with her, standing next to someone I'd actually pay to see perform.

Louise was the main female singer for the show, but they brought me on to sing two songs while the pros were dancing. It's fair to say I was shitting myself. Pete was in the audience that night and so were my family, so I knew I'd get a few cheers but I was still really worried about the reaction I'd get.

I sang two songs that night. One of them was 'With You' from *Ghost* – that's a really difficult song. God knows why I agreed to do that one, as if I wasn't nervous enough already – and the other one was 'Arms of an Angel' by Sarah McLachlan, a song I've always loved and had sung in the talent task in the *CBB* house with Kristina, my fellow housemate, watching on.

Bearing in mind I was in *TOWIE* at the time, what my manager Jade told me afterwards didn't really come as a surprise. She said she'd overheard people in the audience at the beginning of the night, saying about me, 'What's she doing here? Can she even sing?' Pretty understandable, really. But then when I got out there and opened my mouth, the atmosphere completely changed. Jade said you could have heard a pin drop out there, they were that shocked. What can I say? I do like surprising people.

Then, in the summer of 2017, just when it looked like all I might ever be famous for was shooting my mouth off on reality TV, I got the chance to do what I've always wanted. It was all about hard work and good timing.

Like so many good things in life, I got my musical break when I was least expecting it. It was when I was at my most miserable with Pete. To be specific, I was sitting in a TV studio with a fake smile on my face, because my relationship was going to shit.

It was that night of *Celebrity Juice* I told you about – the one when Pete had called me his ex-girlfriend, and Keith Lemon had cracked loads of jokes about texting – so I wasn't exactly having a laugh. But on the same show, they asked me to sing something. I chose a country song, Carrie Underwood's 'Before He Cheats', and I know I surprised a lot of people that night.

Normally, I'd say no to singing on the spot, but for some reason, my manager Jade had said, 'You need to start singing when people ask, and show them your talent.'

I bumped into Louis Walsh backstage afterwards, and he said straight away, 'You should go to Nashville, and get a film crew to go with you.' Jade had been saying the same thing for ages, but I'd never thought anyone would really want to do that for me. Now I was hearing the same thing from someone huge in the music industry, and I thought, 'That has always been my dream.'

Apart from me and Pete digging at each other all night, I had my share of luck. Some ITV producers were sitting in the audience for the show, and they said they were impressed with what they'd heard. Only a few days later, at the National Television Awards, one of the top guys from ITV came over to me and said, 'You need to have your own show and go to Nashville.' I said, 'Everyone's saying this to me now.' I was thinking by now,

'I really want this,' and my manager set up a meeting the very next week. It all went from there.

The deal was, I had one month to film a show all on my own, write and record music and perform in some of the most famous venues in Nashville. If I could do all this, I would get a single green-lit back in the UK. Literally, my dreams of becoming a music artist were coming true. But, not gonna lie, I was absolutely shitting myself.

Even though everything was still completely shit with Pete at this point, inside I knew this was more important – it was, quite literally, the chance of a lifetime. I had to take it seriously and give it everything I had. So a few weeks later, I was heading to Nashville.

It might seem a bit random – Essex girl does country – but actually, this kind of music couldn't be more perfect for me. Ever since I was little, I've always written down little stories in my diaries. As you might have guessed by now, I've always been really emotional, with a really big heart. Country music gives me a place to tell my stories and share those feelings.

Nashville is about four thousand miles from Essex, but it could literally be on the other side of the universe. That's great because it means it doesn't matter if you've appeared in a load of reality TV shows – they have no idea and they don't care. But it means you have to prove yourself completely from scratch against a whole load of competition.

MOUTHY

In the TV series *There's Something About Megan*, they really highlighted my outsider status – I think the producers really liked the whole 'Essex comes to Nashville' thing – but they didn't have to do that much to exaggerate. I was totally out of place when I first arrived. In the first scenes, you see me struggling with my suitcase, and they even filmed it when my heel got stuck in the escalator at the airport. Now that was embarrassing! I didn't look like a country bumpkin, more like an Essex girl trying and failing to arrive in style.

I really loved it, though. The house I was staying in was absolutely beautiful – it was all wood outside, with loads of balconies and porches, proper Deep South, but inside everything was brand new and modern, so I had the best of both worlds.

The best part was having a bright-red truck. It was far too big for me, but it made me feel like I was in my very own Hannah Montana movie.

I made my first trip to the main downtown strip, and it was not what I expected. I thought it would all be a bit tumbleweed but it was the opposite – absolutely buzzing, with music coming out of every bar. It was at this point I realised I was going to have to up my game if I wanted to make any kind of impression in this town. There's something like sixty live music venues spread over a few city blocks, and the one thing Nashville has plenty of is singer-songwriters. There's huge amounts of competition, which meant I was going to have to come up with something not just impressive, but different. And let's just say, I was definitely different. People noticed my Essex accent a mile off.

My manager had arranged a massive meeting for me with a huge music booking agent. For my meeting with this guy, Nick, I did what I always do when it's a really important occasion – spend hours with the tongs on my hair, naturally. What a waste of effort that was! No air-con in the truck meant my bouncy blow-dry turned into a massive frizz just in time for my meeting. Can I just say, Nashville is one of the hottest places I've ever been. Driving around in a truck with no air-con is hell. I was sweating out of places I didn't know I could sweat.

It turned out my hair didn't really matter for this guy Nick. His agency represents actual icons, I mean real stars like Dolly Parton and Mariah Carey, so I was lucky he even agreed to see me, frizz or not. He didn't treat me gently – why should he? – and he told me what I needed to do. He warned me about the tough crowds all over town – 'they see a lot and they see it often' – and he told me I'd have to win people over. He said, 'There are forty thousand people in this town and they all look great.' But he gave me one of the best bits of professional advice I've ever received. It was, 'Be first or different.'

I was just starting to relax talking to Nick, when he suddenly asked me to sing. Right there, in his office, without any prep or even a warm-up. Fortunately for me, I'd had all those years at Ravenscourt and ArtsEd of doing exactly that. Somehow, despite all those reality TV years in between, my vocal cords knew what to do. Just like riding a bike, right? I stood up and belted something out, and he actually smiled! He admitted he hadn't expected my voice to be that good. But he also said, 'You need to work for this. I'm not going to sign you on the spot.'

The next task was to find a decent guitarist, which meant heading off to the strip to hear some session musicians. I met some weirdos along the way, including real-life cowboys and hillbillies, and then I heard two guys, Greg and Alex, performing in a bar. They were so good, like unreal – the standard in this town is SOOO high – but I finally decided to go for Greg. He was cute, seemed like a really nice guy, and was able to play anything! I also liked his general vibe – he seemed really upbeat, and I thought I might need that if things got a bit tough further down the line. Well, guess what? They did.

The next mission was to find a bar that would accept me for a performing slot. Make a note if you're ever considering a singing career in Nashville – this is MUCH harder than it looks. You'd think bars would be grateful to have free musicians turning up and playing for the crowd. Not so much. Bars book bands months in advance, and I was told, 'You can't just walk in off the street.' I tried a few bars, but it was all getting a bit difficult. Plus, I was starting to cough. Got to love my immune system. Never lets me down! And then it started to rain. And I mean pour down. I was shattered, and then I got a call from Bobby's Idle Hour Tavern. They'd had a cancellation and wondered if I wanted to fill the gap. This was it, my big break! There was only one catch – he said, 'I thought in return you might work a couple of hours?' Okay, let me get this right – so in return for performing for free for your customers, I get to work for you pulling pints as well, also for free? Hmmm. I think we know who has the power in this town. Of course I said yes immediately.

It was time for my first session with Greg, and I couldn't have asked for a better musician. He could play anything I asked him to. It was such an amazing night, singing along with Greg, sitting on this warm terrace with a guitar and a song sheet... nothing like my normal Friday night. By now, back home, I'd be down Faces with my girls, probably getting smashed. Don't get me wrong, I do love all that, but this was better than anything I'd done before. It was magical.

And then – shock! – I got sick. The morning before the day of my gig – okay, to be a bit more accurate, my bar shift with a bit of singing thrown in – my cough got so bad that I had to call for a doctor, and she told me I had bronchitis. I was desperate. I'd worked for years to get this massive chance, and here I was in the middle of Nashville and my voice was going to let me down. Greg came over, and even he, Mr Positive Vibes, went a bit pale when he heard my cough. I heard him telling our producer how worried he was – I couldn't get through a song. Pretty soon, I had to give up and go to bed. Just talking about it to camera made me cry. This was very different from all them tantrums I'd had in reality shows – this was my first real chance at doing my music, and I thought, 'Am I going to blow it because of this bloody illness?'

What didn't get shown on the programme was that my amazing sister Milly flew out to keep me company, look after me and just give me a cuddle. Like I said before, she's not just my sister, she's my best friend.

The day of the gig, I thought to myself – what would Dolly do? So I put on my little black dress and got in my red truck. After all those years in Nu Bar, it was time to pull some more pints. Bobby's was right down one end of Music Row, where some of the biggest ever country songs were actually recorded. Taylor Swift has her studio there, and just across the way is Studio B, where Dolly recorded 'Jolene'.

At Bobby's, they thought it was alien that I couldn't drink beer, but obviously it's because of my allergies. They still thought that it was pretty weird. Being coeliac in Nashville was a struggle, with all the fried chicken. Finally, it was time for me to sing.

I should really have been in bed, and I was sucking cough sweets right up until the moment I got on stage. But as Dolly knows, the show must go on, folks! I went on stage with some other performers and waited my turn. This sort of thing is what every Nashville wannabe has to go through, it's called a Writers Round. I had to sit on stage with three other performers, waiting for my turn to sing, with everyone staring at me. It was terrifying. When it came to my turn, I coughed all the way through the intro – bad start! – but somehow I got through two songs. However ill I was, I was never going to give up on this chance.

What I hadn't realised was that there was someone else in the crowd listening, a lady called Beth Nielsen Chapman. She's a Grammy-nominated songwriter – she's written for Faith Hill, Willie Nelson, all sorts – and before I knew it, she was inviting me to come and do a writing session with her. Literally, I couldn't believe this was happening.

Beth's house was stunning. It looked like a real-life doll's house, but the real magic happened in her writing room. She'd done her homework on me; she'd seen a few tantrums on YouTube and she was hilarious – she just called it 'outrageous stuff'. I told her about my fiery side and my meltdowns, but I said they'd never happened 'until I met boys'. She just said everyone goes through stuff, I'd just done mine publicly. It felt weird telling all this to a stranger, but good as well. It was like having a therapy session. And then her guitar came out, and she asked me to sing whatever was inside me. I was really nervous, but it made me realise this is what the business is really all about.

You do hear quite a few bad stories about the music industry, but this was definitely a positive. I realised it's possible to put a song together from scratch. We played with melody and harmonies, and it was all very professional. For the first time, I started to understand the power of my own voice, and I could put all my feelings and emotions into a song. I could share exactly what I was thinking, without having to shout once.

26

The next day, I had to have a big chat with someone else in the industry, called Allen McKendree Palmer – he's been in the business for decades, and he'd turned up to my gig for some moral support.

Allen had two things to tell me. One: that 'High Heeled Shoes' was the song for me. Agreed! Two: that I needed to get in touch with the kind of people who listen to country music beyond the Nashville bubble. So he sent me to the farm.

Yes, a real-life farm, in case you were wondering. I had to drive to the middle of Tennessee – the middle of nowhere, hours from Nashville – and to top it off, a storm was brewing. There was even lightning. I'd never seen anything like it – it was terrifying. When I got there, a lady was standing at the door with this lantern, and she took me to the 'hayloft, where you'll be sleeping'. I'm not joking you, this was my worst nightmare. It turned out I was staying in an old barn, away from the farmhouse. It was literally like something out of a horror movie. The thoughts going through my head were not normal.

There were little baby lambs and some cows, but also lots of spiders and these huge moths that used to fly about. The toilet was miles away in the main house, and I had to sleep up here on my own. Nah, mate, it ain't happening.

To be honest, the producers weren't happy that I didn't stay on the farm, but honestly I would have ended up having a panic attack if I'd stayed there. I can't even go camping. To be honest, I don't even like getting in my mum's florist van because there's spiders in there. I even made her pull over once to get a spider out the van. So as if I'm going to survive in a hayloft... you having a laugh?

Instead, I stayed back in Nashville and got a good night's sleep, but the next morning I was late for my day's work on the farm. The girl, Sam, was fuming, so she made me shovel shit. At this point, I was thinking, 'Fuck, maybe I should have just slept with the spiders.'

She also took me along for market day, and I watched two farmers sing along to a guitar. Later on, we went to a bar where I met some locals and listened to some more music. And then it was off to a barn dance. It's true what they say, there's music everywhere in that place. I even met someone who'd written a song for one of my idols, Carrie Underwood. They asked me if I knew Prince William. It was the real Tennessee. Allen was right, I did need to experience all this.

My next challenge was performing the American national anthem at a local rodeo. I couldn't believe I even got asked! Allen told me, 'Their ears are going to be on you, their eyes are going to be on the flag, and their hands are going to be on their hearts.' I was absolutely shitting myself at this point. I didn't want to know what would happen if I messed this up.

There were thousands of people at this thing, and some of them had travelled miles to watch the cowboys compete – it's the ultimate all-American experience. Not sure they've ever had an Essex girl doing the honours with the anthem before. I met some real-life cowboys and tried to hide my nerves, but I was absolutely convinced I was going to forget the words to the country's most iconic tune. On top of it all, I really didn't like the way the rodeos went and it upset me how they treated the animals.

I walked onto the field, Greg took off his hat and they all said their prayers. Me, being an Essex twat, wore my brand new Chanel boots, and had to walk across a muddy, dusty arena to get to the middle. Yes, they were filthy. Country 1 – Essex 0.

I was shaking so much, I could barely hold the microphone, but we somehow got going. Bearing in mind there's no music here, me and Greg looked at each other. He was shitting it as well, ha ha. Out of the corner of my eye, I could see the whole audience had their hands on their hearts. It was all as serious as Allen had warned me. From now on, if anyone ever wants to doubt my country music credentials, or if they ask me something like, 'Ever been to America?' I'll be able to say, 'Er yeah, I've actually sung their national anthem at a rodeo. What do you think of that?' So it was definitely worth it. Tip to self: wear sensible shoes.

It was time for my second songwriting session with Beth, and as we started working, I started to feel a bit sorry for Pete.

Yeah, Pete – Pete Wicks, not sure if I've ever mentioned him to you before... Well, he and I were back on by the time I went to Nashville. Yeah, yeah, ridiculous, I know, but at that point, we were all good again. We were back on the rollercoaster. But, hey, at least it gave me good material for my music.

When I'd first planned this trip, Pete and I had been split up, and I'd warned him he'd be appearing in any songs I wrote. After all, I've got to get my material from somewhere, true Taylor Swift style. God I feel sorry for my exes now, ha ha.

Beth told me she wanted me to be really open and honest, and put it all down on paper. I had to be really truthful with her, even though I was once again shitting myself. This was my chance to explain all those times when people had just seen me screaming and shouting, plus all those other times I'd been at home on my own, hurting, crying. Every single line of the song was so personal. I felt safe, though. I had Beth beside me, and she guided me through it, bringing out stuff in me that I didn't know I had. Not gonna lie, I was shitting myself about what Pete was going to say.

Then – don't ask me how! – I got invited to perform at the Bluebird Cafe. Unless you've been to Nashville, you won't know how amazing this is. If you've been to Nashville, there's nothing I need to tell you! The Bluebird is tiny, it's only got about twenty tables in total, but it is THE place. Garth Brooks. Taylor Swift. Faith Hill. LeAnn Rimes. Everyone's been. Big-label scouts come round all the time. It is INTENSE.

Allen had one piece of advice for me: 'Make sure you connect. Use your eyes. Use your song. Let them into your personal space.'

I was even more nervous than I'd been at the rodeo, and the line-up was seriously impressive. Beth went up first and sang a song she'd written twenty years before for her late husband. In the room, you could have heard a pin drop. Then it was my turn, sharing all my Pete Wicks dramas with the Bluebird Cafe crowd, with 'Far Cry from Love'. It wasn't perfect. My chest was still bad, but I gave it my best shot. I also had this thing in my chest that I really thought was my nerves – I couldn't shift it in my song and I was worried it was affecting my singing. It turned out, the real problem was... I needed to burp. Fuck my life! Why now, of all times, did I feel like I needed to burp, when I hardly ever burp anyway?

But Beth was lovely, and Allen told me something important. He said that's what being vulnerable is all about. He said, 'Life is not perfect. It's not walking around with perfect makeup and perfect hair and the right shoes all the time, it's about screwing everything up and learning how to pull yourself up by your bootstraps and go on.'

I did have a bit of a confidence crisis after that Bluebird gig, I'm not going to lie. Everyone was being really nice to me, but I knew in my heart of hearts I hadn't done myself justice, and it bothered me. Then, just when I was considering packing up and going home, I got notice from Nick – the agent I met right at the beginning – that he'd scheduled a showcase for me at the end of the week. This was going to be THE performance that decided whether I got a deal or not. SHHHIIIIT. This was something I'd been waiting for my whole life, and it was going to happen.

Time to get real. I needed four songs to perform in front of some very important people. No more time for messing about.

I started off with some vocal coaching, and that was really helpful. The teacher liked my scales. He said to me that if Miley was in the room, who he'd previously taught, she'd say I smashed it.

More importantly for me, he kept asking me why I wanted to sing. I thought the answer to that was obvious – because I love it, because I like the sound of my own voice, because it's what I've always done! But he wanted more from me. He told me about singing to his own one-year-old baby, and then he asked me to think about who I loved in the audience.

As you all know, my family are my number one, they're everything to me, but this teacher made me really connect all my dreams with how I felt about them. I thought about my parents making sacrifices for me, my nan and granddad finding that extra money to get me through theatre school, and of course I thought about my granddad and all his pride in me.

Ahhh, my granddad... and his belief in me that I was going to become a country singing superstar. Back when I was little, he'd sit in the garden in the big chair, I used to stand and sing to him and he'd give his judgement like Simon Cowell. He'd say things like, 'You rushed a bit.' If he could see me now... He was even better than Simon Cowell. The songs he used to pick out for me were always the right choice.

this page: Shooting my music video for HHS!

Megan McKenna

December 2017

02   The Sugarmill
      Stoke on Trent

03   The Venue Derby

05   Palace Theatre
      Southend

06   Scala London

AEGPRESENTS.CO.UK   AXS.COM
AEG PRESENTS IN ASSOCIATION WITH UNITED TALENT

above: **The queue going round the block at the Scala**

left: **The poster for my tour**

above: **Me, my mum and Milly**

left: **My band!**

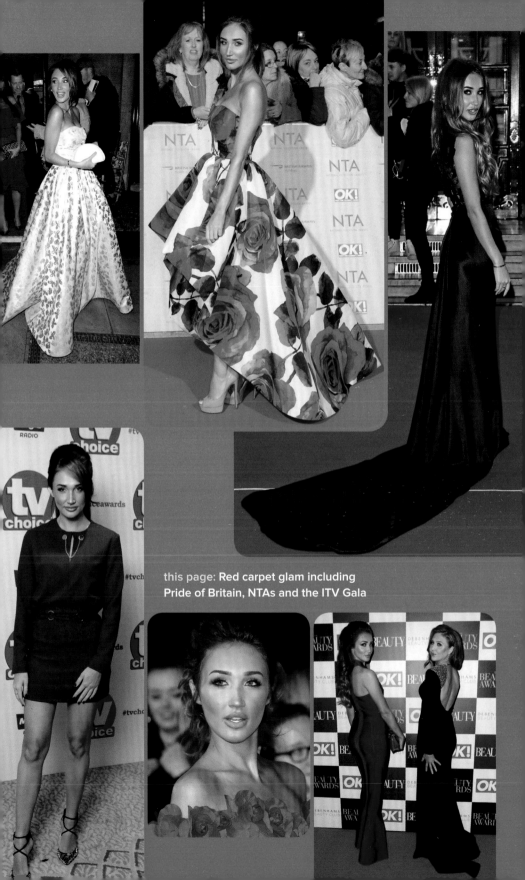

this page: Red carpet glam including
Pride of Britain, NTAs and the ITV Gala

above: Mouthy makeup brand, first shoot

left: Easilocks launch

right: First ever calendar!

MEGAN MCKENNA OFFICIAL 2017 CALENDAR

above: **GMB**

above, right and below: **Singing and winning Best Newcomer at the Boisdale Awards with Jools Holland and Ranald Macdonald**

right: **Me and Amy Wadge**

below: I do love a selfie!

above: The picture I got trolled over for looking like 'I need a wash'

below: another trolled pic over my weight

above: In hospital early 2018!

left: Me and Mike tanning it up in Barbados

below: Dam! Where I fell for Mr Thalassitis

below: We do love a holiday!

right: I love him. X

left: The Calendar Girls shoot

above and below: *The Real Full Monty: Ladies Night!*

The teacher could see me welling up. He said,
'Sing for your granddad, not for yourself. Sing for yourself,
you'll always go wrong. Sing for the song, you'll never
go wrong.'

Meanwhile, any spare time I got, I was doing my
warm-ups like he'd told me. I was even doing my scales
in the car on the way to a photo shoot, where I had to get
changed into a little cowgirl number and swing into action.
Here, for just about the first time in Nashville, I did know
what I was doing.

It was amazing hanging out in Nashville that week. I
visited the Country Music Hall of Fame and saw Elvis's car.
I bought a guitar and had the guy in the shop show me a
chord. I even went to a church on Sunday and watched a
gospel choir sing their hearts out.

That week, I also did a radio interview on a station
called CMT – only ninety million listeners across America!
I'm glad they only told me that afterwards, as I was already
pretty nervous, especially when the DJ, Cody Alan, told
me who else had sat in my chair – yes, turns out Carrie
Underwood had been there, and even Dolly herself.

Cody made me sing as well, but by now I was used to
belting out a tune to order, so I just got on with it.

Finally, the night of the showcase arrived. It was at
the Station Inn, a bit bigger than the Bluebird Cafe but still
pretty intimate. I had an awful last rehearsal with Greg,
and my nerves were definitely getting the better of me.

I even started having a tantrum in the rehearsal. Not a good look! I could see Greg was hiding his impatience. I just thought I sounded rubbish. Once again, this tantrum wasn't about being a spoilt brat, this tantrum was because I wanted it to be perfect – it meant so much to me.

Everything counted on this one night. The agent Nick needed me to pull it off big time at the showcase if he was going to green-light me recording a single back home.

When it came time to walk on stage, I was still feeling the nerves and so was Greg. The place was packed. They were all there: Allen, Nick, plus my mum, who'd flown over from England especially for the occasion.

I wanted to sit there for a bit and take it all in, but there was work to do. I could see Allen's face, and I could see my mum. I just started talking, telling people my story, and then it was time to sing. Pretty much everything I'd ever done, or ever wanted to do, was all going to come down to this moment.

I gave myself a soft warm-up with a cover of a James Bay song, 'If You Ever Want to Be in Love', then up next was my original song, 'Far Cry from Love'. Then came 'High Heeled Shoes', the song I wanted to release if I got the chance.

Finally, I sang 'Fields of Gold', but first, I told the audience about how proud my granddad was of me, how I'd lost him, but how I felt him still watching over me. My biggest fan! He'd have been so proud of this night. I felt really emotional singing it, singing it to him. All the words in that song, I always sing to him.

By the end of the performance, I felt happy. I walked off the stage, gave everyone a hug, and then the agent Nick said he wanted a word.

Once again, he told me straight. He said that at the beginning of my session, people had been chatting and the crowd felt a bit hostile, but as soon as I started singing, they buttoned up. He said, 'They turned silent.'

He told the producers afterwards, 'She opened her mouth and won them over, and that's hard to do.'

Oh, and by the way, he gave the go-ahead for the single's release in the UK. This moment – me standing there with him, him telling me this – made me think everything was worth it. All the hard times, all the crying and all the breakups, had led to my amazing music which everyone loved, so I definitely do believe everything happens for a reason.

I can truly say that trip to Nashville was the making of me. When I first got there, I'm not going to lie, I felt like a bit of a plum. I got bronchitis and I was coughing twenty-four seven. I couldn't pull a proper pint at Bobby's. But the people I got to know were amazing. I hope I get to work with Greg again – he was so patient – plus Allen, who I called my Nashville dad, and Beth, who gave me all that confidence to write.

The whole trip was inspiring – it made me realise that I wouldn't give this up, whatever happened to the single. My granddad used to say that, he used to tell me, 'You never give up.' He would say all the time, 'You will be a star.'

Thanks, Granddad.

As soon as I got back to London, I recorded 'High Heeled Shoes' in a recording studio – which was an amazing experience, getting to work with all these really experienced musicians and producers. Then I just had to wait until the TV series of me going to Nashville aired in September, as the single was going to be released on the back of it. It was really weird knowing I was about to bring out my first single but not being allowed to do any press for it, or talk about it in any interviews, or even mention it anywhere on my social media. I was bursting to say something, but I just had to sit on my hands and keep quiet. To be honest, it did make me go a bit mental, but in a good way!

Finally, after what seemed like ages but was actually only a couple of months, the day the show was going to air came around, and I went on *Loose Women* to talk about it. Obviously, they'd booked me because I was a *TOWIE* face, and the panel did ask me loads of questions about Pete and stuff, but they also asked me all about my music. It did make me feel a bit shy talking about it for the first time, then the next thing I knew, they said, 'Why don't you just sing a bit?'

It was a bit weird, I was literally just sitting there on the panel, not exactly the usual set-up for a musical performance, but I just thought, 'Well, this is my chance to show the nation.' So I sang 'Fields of Gold' – no instruments or accompaniment or anything. I was shitting myself, but even while I was singing, I could see everyone's face changing. That was a really cool moment, because they all seemed genuinely shocked. I don't think any of them thought I had it in me to hold a note. They were all so nice, though, and it was a great thing to do ahead of the show going out later that night.

Literally as soon as the show began airing, I started getting some really nice comments on my Twitter and Instagram – people saying they liked my voice, asking where they could download my music, loads of good stuff. But still I couldn't say anything because that was going to be the big reveal in the very last scene of the series. I just wanted to shout, 'It's coming!'

Finally, three days later, the credits came up for the last show, and then the single got released at midnight that same night. I put one tiny post on my Instagram about it, but that was it. No press, no promo, nothing you'd normally do for a single. I just had to wait and cross my fingers somebody somewhere might download it.

Well, pretty much straight away 'High Heeled Shoes' went into the country chart on iTunes, which I thought was pretty special, but then I saw that 'Far Cry From Love', my own song that I'd written with Beth back in Nashville, was in there as well. Something I'd actually written myself was in the charts. That was even better. I couldn't believe my eyes.

I couldn't think about going off to bed. I was way too excited. Instead, I was just sat in my PJs, watching the iTunes chart on my phone and swapping text messages with my manager Jade. She couldn't sleep either. Then, at about two in the morning, she noticed both songs had gone into the main iTunes chart. AMAAZZING! We were both so busy looking at that, I forgot to look back at the country chart, and then suddenly there I was... at number one AND number two. I was literally screaming! I couldn't believe my eyes. And one of the songs was one I'd actually written myself. What a special moment.

Finally, I dragged myself off to bed and somehow managed to fall asleep. I got back up the next morning, and couldn't resist another quick peek at some point... okay, I'll admit, it was the first thing I did. By now, I was in the top ten of the main chart with both tunes. Not a bad start to the day!

And then, just when I thought that was probably the peak, I went to number one AND two on the main iTunes chart. And knocked Taylor Swift off the top in the process. Sorry, Taylor!

I was still having trouble taking it all in. It didn't feel real. I couldn't believe my own eyes, and I mean, I REALLY couldn't. I was looking at my phone, and I thought it must just be because I had those two tracks downloaded in my phone that I could see them. I thought, 'This can't be true,' so I was ringing round my friends and family, asking them all to check their own iTunes. I remember shouting down the phone, 'CHECK ITUNES!' When they all said they could see it too, it really was OMG.

I can't really explain what it felt like, but here's what I wrote on Twitter that afternoon, and it pretty much covers it. I said, 'OMG I AM OVERWHELMED! I am currently no. 1 & 2 on iTunes! Thank you guys so so much! I love you all for believing in me'. And I meant that, and still do.

Normally, radio stations won't play tracks by reality TV stars, they're like, 'Errr... no,' but because it was that high in the charts, they had to play it. So 'High Heeled Shoes' got played on all of them.

As for the reaction that day on social media, well...
are you ready for this? Not one bad comment, not a single
one, which I have to say was a first for me.

There were no actual plans to make a video, we hadn't
banked on the song doing that well, but because of the
success in the charts we had to quickly put one together.
So I met a bunch of directors, they pitched various
treatments, and I picked the one that felt the most right. I
knew I wanted a proper story to go with the song – got to
do things the proper country way LOL.

Plus, I wanted to feel like I was really in Nashville, even
though when we got to shooting it we were actually in...
Kent. It was a bit more glamorous than it sounds: it was
a full-on film set and loads of big Hollywood stars had
worked there. From the look of it, you definitely would
have thought we were in Nashville.

I had to get up really early to get there and, that
morning, because there was quite a bit of press interest in
me after the song went to number one, I had a pap follow
me all the way from my house in Essex to the location in
Kent, which was hours away. He followed us in his car,
trying to get pictures. Then a few more turned up, so there
were loads of paps buzzing around there in the end, and
it all got a bit crazy and the people on the neighbouring
properties called the police to try and get rid of the paps.
Meanwhile, I was looking at the film set, and I could see

all the cameras, one of them a camera dolly on a mounted track, probably worth a shit load of money. It was so serious and professional. I thought, 'Fuck, this is real.'

But, at the same time, it was amazing. And the best bit was that I had to cast people to feature in it. It was surreal, me sitting there, flicking though all these pages of different models. The boys I chose to play the cowboys in my very own music video were Ollie, Charlie, Chibu and Pamara. It took a whole day and I was shattered by the end of it, but we managed to have a laugh too.

I loved the video. It was everything I wanted, going for that whole country and western vibe. I even got to walk through some wooden swinging saloon doors. I was buzzing, and it makes me smile to this day. The video still gets shown a lot on the music channels and I love seeing it. I always watch it and think, 'WTF? Did that really happen?'

Things just kept building from there. The success of the song and the video led to me doing a mini tour. I started small – just planning two gigs up north, in Stoke and Derby, and then two more down south, in Southend and finishing at The Scala in Kings Cross.

When the tour dates were about to go out, I had all my usual worries – Is anyone going to come? Are there going to be loads of empty seats? What am I going to do with all the leftover tickets? How will I ever be able to show my face? I'd read about how when even a really massive artist can't fill an arena, they hang a black curtain up halfway back in the hall so it looks full. I didn't want to have to ask for the curtain for my very first gig in Stoke.

On the day the tickets went on sale, I tried to distract myself with a trip to Westfields. I'd put one post about the gigs on my social media. I didn't do any other ads, and I was trying my best not to check my phone. Then, I was in Urban Outfitters, standing by the rail, when my mum called me. She said, 'We can't get tickets.' I thought, 'Oh shit, something's gone wrong.' I told her, 'Refresh the page, maybe the link's gone down.' So she tried, but then she said, 'I still can't get any. It says Sold Out.' I thought, 'WTF? This can't be real.' So I phoned Jade to check the website was working properly, and it was. The first tickets had all gone in a few hours, and by the end of the day all four gigs were sold out. The venues even had to release their own production tickets due to the demand. No curtain needed LOL! Phew.

So I went straight into rehearsals and even flew Greg over from Nashville to play in my band, and then it was time to hit the road. The only downside to all this was, because the whole time had been so busy with travelling and rehearsing, plus I was still getting over my bronchitis from Nashville, my voice just gave out. Travelling up to Stoke for the first gig, no one knew but I was having a complete meltdown because I didn't think I'd be able to sing. I got there, though, and got through the first gig in one piece. I gave it my all, but then, when I came off stage, I tried to speak and my voice had completely gone. I thought, 'OMG, what's going on?'

The next day it was even worse. I thought, 'I'm fucked.'

Thank God for my tour manager, Johnny Buckland – love him, I want to give him a massive thank you. If it weren't for him and his medical equipment, a pipe thing for steaming my throat, plus his special emergency medicine mixture, I definitely wouldn't have got through those days. When I wasn't performing I had to go on complete voice rest, and no one was allowed to talk to me, or rather, they were allowed to say what they liked, but I wasn't allowed to answer. I know I must have looked like a right diva sitting there in silence, but trust me, it was the only way I was going to get through it.

But it was all worth it, though. To stand there and see the crowd all there for me, and then to have the whole audience singing back at me, well... I can't explain what it feels like. But it's amazing.

The majority of the songs were covers that I sang in my own style, plus 'High Heeled Shoes' and, guess what, a Miley Cyrus medley. Well, I couldn't leave Miley out, could I?

By the time I got back to London for the final gig at The Scala, I really felt like I was living the dream. For that last one, the queues were going round the block. It felt insane, absolute madness, but it made me realise I was on the right path, that I would be able to do this, even after all that reality TV, because I'd been really worried it would never happen. Reality TV is always going to be something I'll be happy to do, but music is my dream, and if it did have to come down to a choice between the two of them, it's always going to be my music.

It might sound simple moving from that kind of TV show to making music, but it really isn't. Lots of people might try but the problem is, they can't actually sing. I can see why they might think it's easy, starting off in the reality TV world, and instantly getting all that limelight. They probably just think, 'This is easy. I'll do a post here, a post there, do some TV, what's next? Oh, I know, I'll do a single.'

That might be fine for a gimmick, and I could have gone that way myself. I could much more easily have made a pop song and tried to get it played in the clubs, but that's never been what I've wanted to do. Because I've been on TV, I'm lucky I already have a great following so that gives me a step up – and I've worked hard for those followers, just like singers have worked hard for years – but I want to earn my right to be seen as a proper artist. I want to do it the right way, even if it takes a lot more work.

They say the harder you work, the luckier you get. Well, cross my fingers that's true. Before my Christmas gigs, I got signed up by my live booking agent Neil Warnock at United Talent Agency, which was unbelievable. Neil has artists like Dolly Parton and Mariah Carey on his books – he hadn't signed anyone new in five years, but he agreed to take me on. So that meant there were bookings agents in the audience at Christmas, and that set the wheel in motion for summer 2018: supporting Ronan Keating at Rochester Castle, going on stage with a whole load of massive names at the Cornbury Festival – literally performing on the same bill as Alanis Morissette – and the best of all, supporting Michael Bublé at British Summertime in Hyde Park. I think I'm just going to say that again. Michael Bublé. Pinch me!

One of the best things that's happened to me recently is meeting Amy Wadge. She co-wrote 'Thinking Out Loud' with Ed Sheeran, and loads of other amazing songs. I have a really cool bond with her; we just click. I have been to Wales a few times recently to write music with her, and we've come up with songs, recording them straight away in the studio.

Amy's a perfectionist, but so am I; it's probably why we get on so well. I'm very fussy, and I want to make sure the songs I'm singing relate to me. I want all my music to feel as personal as possible.

So that's the plan going forward – gigging, writing, getting my stuff out on Spotify, putting out some acoustic tracks, building up my following, and proving to people that I'm serious about this. I know I've had some amazing chances to get this far, but the real work starts now.

My biggest pinch-me moments

💋 The time I was a question on *The Chase.* They asked, 'Megan McKenna became a regular in which reality TV series?' This was always my granddad's favourite show, and it made me think for that second, 'Fuck, I've really made it.'

💋 The moment I was standing behind the Eye to walk into *Celebrity Big Brother.* I've always been a massive fan of the show, and suddenly I was in it

💋 Getting three Yeses on *Britain's Got Talent* when I was only sixteen, from the judges Simon Cowell, Amanda Holden and Piers Morgan

💋 Nine years later, Piers Morgan asking me for a pic for his Twitter when I was a guest on *Good Morning Britain*

💋 Meeting Simon Cowell for the first time. And yes, he's really nice. Nothing like as nasty as he used to come across on screen, although he smiles a lot more these days. Big softy, really!

💋 Four thousand people in Wembley Arena chanting my name because they thought the judges made a mistake getting rid of me from the Six-Chair Challenge

💋 Getting a blue tick on Instagram and Twitter

💋 Getting a number one slot on the main iTunes chart. Knocking off Taylor Swift – sorry, Taylor!

💋 Making my first music video – I'd dreamt of this literally since I was a little girl

💋 Getting the keys to my first home

💋 Standing in the middle of a rodeo in Tennessee, singing 'The Star-Spangled Banner' in front of a load of actual cowboys

💋 Standing six rows from Justin Bieber at the O2. He was singing. I was only in the crowd but I could literally see his armpit hair

💋 Cheryl Cole following me on Twitter

💋 Getting Best Newcomer for my music at the Boisdale Awards

💋 Supporting Michael Bublé at British Summertime Hyde Park

💋 Looking at the hot tub in my very own back garden. Come on, sun!

💋 The staff in McDonald's in Liverpool letting me go behind the counter and serve people, and even letting me have a free Maccy D's

28

So now I need to rewind a little bit, and tell you what happened when I got back from Nashville, in time for filming the next series of *TOWIE*, the one that would end up being my final one. Pete and I were once again hanging by a thread. By the middle of the series, we were both bored, both getting frustrated and both definitely ready to call it a day.

A few times by then, things had come up about our past flings or shit written in the press, and I would always say to Pete, 'Tell me everything.' But I just felt like he never learned his lesson.

This, for me, was the actual problem. This was what I could never get with Pete – every time we had any kind of drama in the press or even just between us, if he'd just been truthful with me from the start, there wouldn't have been any agg. Nothing major happened, but to me small things like that just got too much.

Finally, we sat down on camera and I said, 'We just don't work. I do want you to be happy, but I want to be happy, and I feel like we're not.'

And Pete agreed: 'All we did was row.'

What no one knew was that we'd already had this chat between ourselves a week before, so it was doubly awkward to go through it again for the cameras. I'd already made my decision about what I wanted, and that was calling it a day with Mr Wicks.

So for me and Pete, that really was it. I mean, REALLY really. After all those arguments, the screaming matches in the street, the breaking up, the making up, we were actually properly finished. It was sad, really, as we had always got on so well – okay, apart from the times when we hadn't. You know what I mean. For possibly the first time in my life, I found myself being able to make the right decision about leaving a boy. But, as any girl who's been hurt and messed up in the head will know, that isn't always the best time to make any other decisions.

29

The thing about us girls is, we just don't get over stuff, do we? Especially not as quickly as boys might like us to. Pete could never understand why I couldn't just put all that messaging shit behind me, but it proper hurt. Plus, because I'd never got over everything properly in the past, my disastrous time with Pete didn't heal me. It actually did the opposite – it opened up all the old wounds, brought back all the hurt I'd felt over The Dip and stupidly sent me running back to him.

If Pete and I had treated each other normally and nicely, and then just grown apart, it might have all fizzled out gradually. I'd have grown up, carried on doing my own thing, gone on another show, whatever. Instead, I was propelled back to those Nu Bar days, and to how bad I felt throughout that time. I definitely felt like I had something to resolve from them days. Let's be honest, I never really got over The Dip, probably because I covered it all up by being on the telly, jumping from boyfriend to boyfriend, getting smashed every night, screaming my head off and then going out with Pete. What I SHOULD have done was go to therapy, learn why I let myself down all those times in Nu Bar and beyond, been fully single for a while and then finally done some telly. Oh well, live and learn and all that.

Soon after Pete and I officially called it a day, I rang The Dip and said straight away, 'I want to talk to you.' I told him I loved him. I never said I wasn't dramatic!

It must have been a weird call to get. I hadn't spoken to him in ages. I hadn't even been in contact with him since our reunion in Sheesh all those months before, but it was time. I don't know why I chose now, but that's how it happened.

I said, 'I can't stop thinking about you. I have dreams about you.'

He said, 'Do you want to come over?'

Just like that, me and him began again. We had a chat, went for a dinner and got spotted. And so, before we'd even paid the bill, we'd given everyone something to talk about and, once more, my private life was about to become very, very public.

Being on *TOWIE* was getting harder and harder for me. Ever since I'd started, I'd always been painted as the bad girl, so this was the perfect opportunity for all those people who'd never been my biggest fans to tell Pete, 'Told you so.'

Meanwhile, he was sitting there, looking all hurt, venting about me getting back with my ex-boyfriend so quickly. He accused me of throwing him under the bus, telling everyone, 'Only one of us was in this properly,' which wasn't true at all, I did give my all to that boy, but there was nothing I could say.

It was also quite bad luck from the timing aspect, and frustrating because they just kept focusing on 'Poor Pete'. Plus, other people kept talking to the papers, saying the cast were 'turning on me'. Sorry to say, but that was bollocks! The cast had never turned to me to begin with.

Another problem for me was that I always made good drama on that show. People who didn't even know me piped up with their opinions, cos they knew it would get them airtime. There was some new girl – desperate to get herself some attention – who suddenly came out with this stuff, saying she'd seen me and my ex out for dinner 'all over each other'. Firstly, I'm not someone who does PDAs, and secondly, she didn't even know me – she didn't know what I'd been going through with Pete, or when it ended. But she still had her little moment, slagging me off. Oh well, good luck to her!

And then bloody Gatsby threw in his oar, saying he had 'evidence' I'd cheated on Pete. Evidence?

Unbelievable. And then Arg apparently confirmed it. What? I couldn't believe all these people were busy making up stuff about me. Even The Dip himself gave these boys a phone call, clearing it up, that I had not cheated on Pete with him.

Pete couldn't help himself, either, telling Lockie, 'The more I hear, the more closure it's giving me.' It was like there was this great pile of betrayal by me that he was slowly uncovering. The whole thing just made me sick to my stomach.

I did whatever I could to defend myself. I explained to the girls, 'I'm single, I went for dinner with my ex-boyfriend and I had a good time. I haven't done anything wrong.' At least I waited until I was single, unlike Pete.

I wanted to scream at them, 'I was a good girlfriend, I didn't cheat, I got hurt, I cried so much over that boy. Now, I'm just enjoying myself. I'm going for a bit of dinner.'

Meanwhile, Pete had his Oscar-winning moment with Lockie. He said to him, 'The more stuff I hear and the more you look back on something... I've wasted two years of my life feeling like shit. I'm half the geezer I was, I've allowed myself to be dictated to and act in a way that's never me by someone who's not worth it in the first place. I don't want to see her, I don't want to hear about her, fuck her.'

It made me so angry. I really did try with him. He fucked up. End of.

Meanwhile, The Dip... well, obviously, we were back in touch and doing our own thing in private. He apologised for everything that had happened before, for being too young and seeing me all heartbroken. He apologised for not being grown up when it mattered.

Basically, The Dip sold me the dream. It was all very romantic – it felt like we were back in love and this was how things were always meant to be. I was staying with him a lot, he was saying all the right things, and then...

It's hard to put into words. He seemed to be living the same life we'd been living before, but I'd changed. I had a wake-up call one morning, and thought, 'That's not my life. I've grown up. I haven't gone through all of that for this.'

Also, a few articles had come out, by some fame-hungry girl, saying he'd left her for me and they'd been texting. He said she was lying, and of course I believed him. A few other things happened, I felt like he hadn't changed and I was just so over it and drained by now that we broke up.

I left his house, and, normally I would've been running back, possibly a bit drunk, probably shouting, demanding to be let back in, but this time I just didn't want to. I'd kept the fire burning for him all that time, had wanted him for so long, but now I had him, I just didn't want it. It felt like a weight had been lifted off my shoulders.

I know I needed to go back to him to find out for sure, and it made me realise two things. One: that Pete wasn't the right person for me. And two: that I had truly loved The Dip, but I didn't love him any more. I'd grown up, he hadn't, and now we were in two different lanes, so it was never going to work. It was sad, but it was done.

I left his house, and he didn't come out. I realised that could be my other life – me always knocking at his door to sort it out, still basically knocking at that same door after all these years. And I couldn't. I phoned my mates and said, 'No more.' They didn't believe me for a while. Fair enough!

At that point, I did take myself off to therapy. It was helpful offloading all my shit, especially to someone totally independent. It also gave me a chance to clear my brain, and it reminded me of what I really want in my life, which is to be creative and successful through my music.

Would I recommend therapy? Definitely, but I'd also recommend hanging out with your mates, your family, the people you totally trust. It all helps.

30

One of the things I appreciate the most about the way my career has developed in the past year is getting invited to take part in things I wouldn't have dreamed of when I was younger.

Even with all the things I've done over the past few months – feeding animals on a farm, singing the US national anthem in front of loads of cowboys at a rodeo – something really special that stands out for me is *The Real Full Monty: Ladies Night*, a once-in-a-lifetime experience that I'll always remember.

I'd heard all about the boy version the year before – a bunch of male celebs stripping off to raise awareness of prostate cancer – so when I heard they were planning a ladies' one, I really wanted to take part. My granddad

suffered from prostate cancer, so I thought this would
be a really nice way of paying tribute to him. I also knew
it would be a great show, an opportunity to meet some
amazing people and work with them, and it was a really
important cause too – raising awareness of breast cancer
as well as other types of the disease.

I went for a meeting with the producers in London,
and they were keen for all of us taking part to have some
sort of connection to the illness – sadly, there aren't
many families that don't – but when I got there, I kept
asking loads of questions, and I think they realised I could
be useful on the show like that as well. They needed
someone to be a bit thick – and I don't mean that in a
bad way at all, I just mean someone who wanted to learn
stuff – and I was happy to be that person. I wasn't shy
about asking, 'What does that mean? What does that look
like?' which meant I could help loads of viewers who were
probably wondering the same thing. Plus, they wanted
to reach a younger audience who'd be asking those
questions too, and it was really important for me to be able
to do that. I hope I did bring in some younger viewers, just
like my friend Arg hopefully did on the boys' one.

So I went for this big meeting, dressed up all nice, and
had these big chats about the show and how it would all
work, and finally I remembered to ask about the actual
clothes we'd be wearing, or I should say, lack of them. I
asked whether they wanted us to bare all, and the answer

was, 'Whatever you feel most comfortable baring.' For some reason, I asked them, 'Will I be able to wear nipple tassles?' like I thought that was going to make it look any better LOL.

I remember thinking I'd probably end up in some sort of sexy suspender underwear, complete with nipple tassles! – don't ask me why! – like it was going to be a cabaret-type thing, some sort of burlesque outfit. They kept saying, 'It's for you to discuss with the other ladies,' so I just thought, 'Oh, that'll be fine, we'll sort it out... and I'll definitely be wearing nipple covers.'

I got the official yes a few days later, which was amazing. A few months passed before we were set to begin rehearsing. I got busy and forgot to think much more about it really, until the day before the very first rehearsal, when they rang me to check, 'Are you ready for tomorrow? It's going to be exciting meeting everyone.'

I was in the car when they rang and I replied, 'Cool, I just want to double check. I'm going to be wearing nipple covers, right?'

Big pause.

They said, 'No, this is actually going to be baring all.' I said, 'What, not my nipples?' but they said, 'Well, yeah.' I thought, 'What have I gone and done here?' but they explained that, when we went completely topless, all the TV viewers would see would be our backs, so that made me feel a bit better, even though I soon realised there'd be a live audience there as well who'd be getting an eyeful of a lot more.

I also started panicking about the rehearsals as well. It wasn't just going to be the girls in the room, there'd be all the film crew, producers, everyone looking. I didn't sleep much that night.

I got to the rehearsal room the next day and we were all introduced. Such a lovely group of ladies, and a huge mixture – presenters Victoria Derbyshire, Sarah-Jane Crawford and Coleen Nolan, Sally Dexter from *Emmerdale*, legend Ruth Madoc, comedian Helen Lederer, plus popstar Michelle Heaton and me.

When it came to getting our kit off, some people were braver than others, they just got on with it, getting their boobs out, practising the dance steps, but I couldn't do that. I said, 'I'm not doing it until the last possible moment,' even though loads of people kept telling me, 'It'll be better for you just to get them out and get used to it,' but I couldn't. I kept saying 'No' and I stuck to my word.

Throughout the rehearsals, it did get difficult, especially when they threw things at us at the last minute, like photo shoots where we had to strip off. Don't get me wrong, I've done those kind of sexy photo shoots before where you're clearly not wearing much even if you can't see anything, but I'm not a topless model and, well, I've not got the biggest boobs and I've definitely got the smallest boobs out of the group, so it got quite difficult for me. One day we did a Calendar Girls shoot where we covered up our bits with cakes, buns and bottles of champagne. To be fair, I only need a couple of cup cakes for mine! But, although I've got this massive grin on my face in the pictures, in reality I ended up going off camera and having a little cry. I know it might sound silly, but I just felt really exposed and self-conscious. I just kept thinking, 'I know the viewers aren't going to see much, but there are so many other people in this room!'

What made it worse for me was knowing that what some of those other girls had been through was so much worse than any of this. Victoria and Michelle had both been through mastectomies, they'd been frightened for their lives, and there was me worrying about just showing them off. Trust me, I absolutely knew it was stupid but it didn't stop me feeling like that.

Apart from my small boobs, I've got other insecurities about my body. People might not realise, but I worry about things like my waist, my legs, and I was worried about the film crew seeing all that. At one point, they were filming us from all angles while we were rehearsing, and I asked them, 'Oh, can you not shoot me from the back?' They must have been thinking, 'What on earth is she going on about?' But that's the real me, always panicking.

I know I have lots of photos of my body out there, but when I'm taking pics for Instagram, it's always in a very private, controlled setting. There are normally only a couple of people there, and they are ones I know and trust – like my manager, makeup artist, hairdresser and our photographer Danny Craven, who I've worked with for a long time now and have built up a friendship with – but in this situation there were loads of people wandering around that I didn't know at all, and it completely threw me.

This is how insecure I got. At one point, I even went and got a mirror to check my reflection, and I got absolutely slated online for worrying about my hair and stuff. People were writing, 'There's people on there that have really suffered, get over yourself.'

The difference between me and the other ladies, though, is how much shit I have to read, daily, about myself online. I get trolled a lot more than the others because I'm of that age where it happens a lot more frequently. Who in their right mind is going to troll Ruth Madoc? It shouldn't happen to any of us, actually, but I've got a large younger following and, while most people are lovely, that's where the trolls are, let's face it.

I should tell you it does make me worry when I put pictures on Instagram. Only the other day I was about to put a nice picture up there, and then I realised it looked, to me at least, like I had a bone sticking out a bit. No one else noticed, but I was worrying the whole time, asking,

'Do you think someone's going to say something?' I was over-analysing the whole thing so much that, one point, I thought, 'I'm just not going to put the picture up,' before I realised I was being stupid. But my fear comes from all the trolling.

I knew *The Real Full Monty* would be a big chance for them to get at me, so I was a bit wary. It stayed on my mind the whole time I was rehearsing for the show. It was a big shadow hanging over me, just waiting for the backlash, waiting for the shit to hit the fan, but I'm stubborn, so I was never going to give up. I wouldn't give them the satisfaction, plus it was far too important.

I say never giving up, but... there was a moment on the very first day when I thought I wouldn't be able to manage it. Never mind the boobs, it was the dance steps that were the problem. As you know, I've had stage training for years, but as you also know, dancing was never my strong point back in the day. Lovely Ashley Banjo was teaching us the routine but, not going to lie, after that very first session, I got in the car, came straight home and told my mum, 'I can't do it. I can't pick up the routine. I don't know if I want to go back. I feel embarrassed.'

My mum made me a cup of tea and then did exactly the right thing. She said, 'Show me the routine. Show me all this stuff you can't do.' So I went through it, and she just laughed. She said, 'There's nothing wrong with that. Pull yourself together.'

The other thing that changed my mind was getting a text message that night from Coleen Nolan. What a nice woman! She could see I was over-thinking everything, and really beating myself up over the steps in the rehearsal, so she sent me a lovely message, telling me how good I looked, and adding, 'We're all in this together.' I really didn't know Coleen that well at that point, but it came at just the right moment, and it was really kind of her.

We had ten days of rehearsal in total, spread out over a few months, and my confidence really grew after that first session. It was like being back at stage school for me. I used to turn up to rehearsals early, and all us ladies became very close too.

I hadn't known any of the others that well before we did this. Victoria was really strong, very nice, I got on really well with her. Coleen became like my rehearsal mum, looking out for me all the time. Helen and I used to stand together at the back, giggling our way through the rehearsals, trying to help each other out. I also got really close to Sarah-Jane, such a cool girl. She's vegan, I'm gluten-free, so we became 'the difficult pair' at lunchtime together. She's become a great friend.

One day, we were all invited to attend the Moulin Rouge cabaret in Paris, which meant travelling by Eurostar, and I ended up sitting with Ruth. She and I hadn't had a chance to chat properly until then; she probably had no idea who I was – can't blame her for that – and neither did

I realise how much work she'd done. She was telling me all the different roles she'd played, including playing Daffyd's mum in *Little Britain*. Well, that made me totally starstruck. I LOVE that show! Of course, I told her that, and then she asked me what I'd been up to. I told her a few stories – managed to leave out most of the bad language – and she was hilarious about it all. She couldn't believe all the dramas I'd gone through in my young life. She sat there with her mouth wide open and eventually she said, with perfect comic timing in her brilliant Welsh accent, 'Well, I learn something new every day.'

When we got to the Moulin Rouge, well... I have to say, I thought the dancing was pretty average, but then I guess people don't really go for the dancing. The room itself was amazing, though, like being on the set of *Bugsy Malone*. We were all there to get our confidence up apparently, to realise that everyone gets their boobs out, it's no big deal. But... the difference with those girls is, they're cast specifically to look a certain way; they have to have a regulation body, height, weight, everything, plus, if you can hold a pencil under your boobs, you don't get the job – I'd actually pass that test! – whereas we were all different shapes and sizes. Oh well, keeps it interesting, I suppose.

For the night itself, we all had to go up to Sheffield to film it, and it's fair to say that, by the time we got to the theatre, the adrenalin was pumping. In our dress rehearsals, we'd had people's tops pinging off and I was feeling the nerves all over again. When we got to our final rehearsal, I was pinging my top off but I was actually secretly wearing another bra underneath, as I still couldn't bring myself to do it. The crew lit us deliberately so that we'd be less exposed, but a lot of people could still see us, I'm sure.

By the time it came to get out there for real, I was so nervous my mouth completely dried up. Literally, my lips were sticking to my veneers, ha ha.

Despite all that, I have to say, it was really good fun getting ready – getting all glammed up with the other ladies, plus my makeup girl Sam really smashed it. This is a special shout out to Sam for that night; she'd literally just had her baby but she knew how important the night was, so she came all the way to Sheffield to do my hair and makeup – I love that girl, I want her everywhere with me. I just want to roll her up and keep her in my bag. She's magic!

After all that worry, the routine itself went off perfectly. Okay, we made a few mistakes along the way, some of us forgot some bits, but we got through it in one piece, thanks to some clever camera angles, and the massive smiles on our faces at the end were all completely genuine. We had the best time. When the song 'This is Me' from The Greatest Showman comes on, it still gives me goosebumps.

A huge support to me that evening was having my family around me, plus a very special someone at my side for the whole thing. Along with everyone else, he travelled all the way to Sheffield to make sure I was all right, and support me through the night. But I'll get to him in a bit...

Why did doing *The Real Full Monty* matter so much to me? Well the whole performing side of it was something I hadn't shown to the public for a really long time, so I thought lots of people were going to be saying stuff like, 'What's she going to be like? Is she going to be any good? Will she be rubbish? What's she doing there?' That was a big thing for me, plus I was stressing out so much about getting my boobs out that when I finally did it, it felt like a really big achievement.

I think lots of people look at me and think, 'Oh, it's that nutter on the TV,' but this show gave me a chance to show people I'm just a normal, insecure girl, just like anyone else my age.

Plus it was a major-league big show, an important, serious message, with me standing on stage next to people I'd never thought I would work with, people like Coleen and Ruth. But like Coleen said, we really were all in it together. We got on so well, we formed a GroupChat and we're all still in it, chatting away. I've done group TV before and what normally happens is, you form a GroupChat and then one by one everyone leaves it over the next couple of weeks and that's it, you don't speak again, but not this time. This experience definitely meant something to all of us.

The reaction to our performance was amazing. On the night itself, my social media went nuts and it didn't calm down for weeks. Most importantly, we had messages from all sorts of people, including young girls, saying that, for the first time, it had made them check their breasts.

One viewer wrote to me, and this is what she said:

'I just want to say a massive thank you for saving my life. After *The Real Full Monty* was shown on TV, I checked my breasts, which is something I never do. I was devastated to find a lump. The following day I was seen by a doctor and referred to a breast clinic. This week I have received the devastating news I have breast cancer. Never did I think at thirty-eight this would happen. I'm now due to have surgery and have a full mastectomy. Thankfully by catching it early I have a good chance at life. Thank you from the bottom of my heart.'

I was stunned to receive this message, and so relieved she'd got checked early. Because the truth is, young girls don't check. They don't think it's going to happen to them. Especially girls with small boobs like me. So it's really, really important.

On a personal note, I was pleased to have the chance to show this other side of myself. The whole experience taught me that it's okay for me to feel scared about stuff, but, as long as I keep going, I'll be able to do more things that feel well outside my comfort zone.

And, after that little bit of abuse about the mirror early on, all the trolling stopped. I didn't get one nasty comment. It was all positive. So that was another learning experience, just another one to add to the many.

31

Hmmm... I'm guessing you guys have got this far by now and are maybe wondering if I'm going to mention a certain someone?

My very own Greek god, ha ha. Mike Thalassitis. You may know him better as Muggy Mike from *Love Island*. But to me, he's definitely not muggy. For one of our first proper dates, he whisked me away to Amsterdam for a romantic weekend. I know you guys were thinking, 'Who is she away with?' when you saw my pictures but, for once in my life, I knew this was something special and I really wanted to keep it to myself. Yeah, I probably could have swerved putting the rose petal picture on Instagram, but I was genuinely so excited, and I just had to share it. Come on, who doesn't like a little fairytale?

It wasn't long before a few people saw us out there and it soon got to the papers. I suppose this is the game we're both in, but it didn't ruin our time away. It was the most romantic break I've ever had.

By the time we got back from Amsterdam, I'm not going to lie, I'd already fallen, and fallen hard. Naturally, we just started to see each other every day, and up to now, apart from the odd work thing here and there, we've not spent a day apart.

As you can see from my Instagram, we do both love a holiday. So far, we've been to Barbados and Cyprus, and our pictures usually get splashed over the papers. The thing that really bugs me is when I see comments saying things like, 'Surely this is fake,' or 'Really? They're only going to last two minutes.'

Well, all I can say to those people is, I haven't had the best luck in relationships, so I'm not about to give my heart to something that's not genuine.

The good thing is, he's come along at a time when I am determined to not have my private life quite so public any more, and he feels the same. We're not one of those couples that needs to be out and about, being seen, we keep ourselves to ourselves, and one of the things I love best about being with him is that we don't need to be doing something glamorous to have the best time.

Like, we have these little cooking nights. Yes, he loves to cook. And if any of you follow me on Snapchat, you know I love to cook too. So we have our little nights, cooking dinner, playing music and trying out new recipes. (He even makes me gluten-free fried chicken, what a keeper!)

We also love to party, and there's nothing better than being out with him, him being taller than me, putting his arm around me, and making me feel like I'm the only girl in the room. One of our favourite things is dancing to MK, and I'd definitely say '17' is our favourite song. Weird shit keeps happening with that song. Recently, I was at my restaurant and it came on. So obviously I voice-noted it to Mike, as you do, and he called me straight away. He said, 'That's so weird, I was just singing that song, thinking of you.' It's the little things, but these little things keep happening. Would you call that fate? I would.

And it's not just the song thing, trust me, there have been loads of things like that. Sometimes I sit there and think, 'Wow, how many signs am I going to get that this is meant to be?'

What else can I tell you? The way we kiss, it's just... UNREAL. We just click, and I feel lucky that someone I love this much treats me so well and loves me the same back. I was starting to think, 'Am I ever going to find that? Surely I deserve it.' But now I have it, and there are loads more memories I want to make with this boy. He's everything I ever dreamed of. It's true what they say. If you don't know what you've got until it's gone, it's definitely also a case of, you don't know what you've been missing until it arrives.

32

Before I went to Nashville, I had loads of belly problems
– I saw a specialist and got diagnosed with IBS on top of
my coeliac condition. I started feeling unwell, lost loads
of weight and couldn't hold anything down. Complete
nightmare. Basically, I got the shits twenty-four seven.

This meant I got really skinny. I'm skinny already, don't
get me wrong, but this was extra wrong. It didn't help
that when I got to Nashville I got bronchitis because my
immune system was low. While I was there, I uploaded a
picture of me in a sparkly dress, and the abuse I got was
vile: really nasty stuff about me having anorexia, all the
same stuff I got back at school.

Could someone please tell me, I'd really like to know,
why is it okay to call someone anorexic, skeletal or gaunt,

but you can't call someone fat or chubby? Even recently, after losing even more weight from being in hospital, I look at my body and I look really skinny, but it's never through dieting. I know my pictures have ended up sometimes on anorexia websites, and I just wish people could leave me alone.

It's not good for me and it's not good for anybody. I'm not dying. I've had problems my whole life with my stomach – I eat a lot, but if I'm unwell, I can't keep anything in, and for a long time, no one understood this.

I want people to see I'm normal, but I get trolls sending me these messages not thinking I have any feelings. I wake up to lots of great messages, and that's lovely, but I also get a lot of nasty stuff every single day.

Recently, I was in my own restaurant, wearing a puffer jacket, and it all started up. That's me, on a Saturday afternoon, in my own restaurant, not wearing any makeup, for fuck's sake. I can't win. If I look too glam or I'm in a bikini, it's 'She's a fucking slut,' but if I'm in my puffer jacket, it's 'She's a mess. She looks like she needs a wash.'

I'm pretty tough these days, but I'd say the odd thing can still get to me. Only this week, somebody sent me a spiteful message about my lips, saying they'd distorted my face. I wanted to put it on my Instagram and bait this girl's life up, and I was so close to doing it, but instead I left it. (Wow, I'm actually learning for once!)

It played on my mind a little bit, I have to admit – it just sounded so bitter – but then I thought, 'This girl clearly ain't got a life.'

The worst time was when my granddad died, and people were going, 'Well, you're such a scumbag from being on TV, he deserves to rot in his grave.' I think it's fair to say that bothered me. I wouldn't be human if it didn't. That's possibly the worst comment I've ever had.

The odd one I might reply to with something comical, and then everyone supports me. But I've got tougher, 100 per cent tougher. I'm a lot tougher than I ever realised I could be, from going through all this shit. Every day something kicks off – there's a drama of some sort, either an article or someone saying something. I guess you just get used to it.

I know people say I signed up for this, and it's true I signed up for lots of other things, but I didn't sign up for abuse. No one's perfect, everyone makes mistakes. I'd just like people to give me a bit of a break sometimes, because I'm actually pretty down to earth.

I don't care about all the VIP stuff – special tables, perks like that. I don't want to be standing somewhere cut off. I just go out with my mates at the weekend and mix with everyone. If I'm not dressing up for some event, I'd much rather put on a pair of leggings, a bomber jacket and a cap. That's the real me. I've always been a bit of a chav, LOL.

People see me on *TOWIE* all glammed up – you're not allowed to wear tracksuits while you're filming anyway, they expect a certain level of effort – and I do like dressing up, but in reality my whole wardrobe is tracksuits, caps and trainers. I'm a lot more of a tomboy than people think. Away from the glamorous places, I hardly ever wear makeup in the day, only at weekends.

I don't really miss my privacy – I only miss it when it comes to relationships, when I'm feeling a bit vulnerable anyway, like any girl would. I generally think that if people want to write stuff, they can. I can happily walk down the street. I get looks, which I try to ignore. I try not to give any eye contact, because if I give back even a glimpse, I think they'll start on me – they'll think I want a fight, because of how I come across on TV.

These days, though, it's more likely to be girls coming up to me and telling me, 'I love you. You're a psycho and I'm like that. You're just like me. I have a meltdown all the time, and you're the only girl who's behaved like that on TV.' It's a funny thing to be known for. So while the older generation might look at me and think, 'scum', to these younger girls, I'm expressing all the anger they're feeling. Everyone has meltdowns.

To give you a rough idea, I'd say about 10 per cent of the attention I get is negative. I've been called all sorts of things in my time; I've been shouted at. On nights out, girls have wanted to start a fight with me. It's all made life a lot harder. I get lots of invitations to nice things, I'm very lucky, but I constantly have to watch my back. It's scary, because I've always got that thing on my shoulder.

I went to a personal appearance up north – not to be confused with the one where I got the bottle thrown at me – and we had to get extra security because someone was threatening to stab me. I just think, 'You never know.' This person could hate me. You do get these fruit loops around the place, and I have this fear, whenever I go out. I'll admit, there's a tiny part of me waiting for someone to punch me. They know me, but I don't know them. Some people turn up outside a venue, and I think, 'You could be one of the trolls that hates me, and I would never know.' I'm always nice, but if I feel any kind of weirdness in the situation, I'll start walking.

It's a small price to pay, though, for all the things that have come to me in the last few years. I've been invited to amazing events and met all sorts of amazing people – it's been an overwhelming couple of years. Plus, I've had the chance to build business collaborations like I never would have imagined. One thing I want to say about them, though, is that anything I put my name to, it has to be authentic. I need my name to be there for a reason.

So, for example, the reason I wanted to launch a range of hair extensions is that I know not everyone can afford them. I kept getting my extensions done at Easilocks, and we spoke about doing a Bouncy Blow in a hairpiece. My fan base is young girls, and they're always sending me messages asking about my hair. Lots of them want hair like mine, but they can't afford it. I remember when I was at Nu Bar, a full head of hair extensions cost something like £700. I could never find that kind of money, so I wanted to make a hairpiece that young girls can buy without breaking the bank. I wish there'd been a girl like me, releasing something affordable, when I was their age.

It's the same reason I did Mouthy, my makeup brand. I'm old enough to get lip fillers now, but I can remember all those years of wanting to try stuff out. It's why I came up with lip kits. When I was younger, I'd have loved my own lips to look bigger without filler, so that's why I did a UK version of Kylie Jenner's kit. I put the first ones on sale and they all sold out in one day. Crazy! Girls really want this stuff. Then, people kept asking me where I got my tracksuits from, so I thought, 'I need to do a line,' which has now led to my very own line – Studio Mouthy. All of this is me. I could never just sign up for something I didn't care about.

One of the biggest things I've created is my own restaurant, McK Grill in Woodford. That came about because I go to loads of restaurants and it's always a load of hassle – they have hardly anything gluten-free or wheat-free. So I thought I would open a place where you can have anything you like without having to worry about that stuff. Whatever you want – waffles, mac 'n' cheese,

roast beef and Yorkshire pud, it can all be wheat-free.
I chose Woodford because it was a nice little spot and
those are my roots.

Who knows what the future will bring? I'm hoping it's
going to involve lots of singing, writing and touring. I've
always said I want to be on the road, and that's never
changed. My dream is still that big tour bus. Dolly's is pink,
but mine would be blacked out, modern, with a bit of bling
here and there. It's all designed in my head.

You have to dream big, and my dreams are still really
big. If my music works out, and it's down to me, I'd like to
live half the time in America – maybe get an apartment
somewhere – but always be based here. My home will
always be Essex.

I do want to get married and have kids, but I want to
have my career first. Ideally, I'd have the kids, they'd come
to my shows and I'd get to bring them on stage. When
people ask me where I see myself in ten years' time, my
answer is, 'Touring the world, singing my own songs to an
army of fans.' I've been working on this my whole life, and I
will live this dream.

33

I've learnt so many lessons during these past few years, most of them the hard way. Is there any other way, come to think of it?

Rule number one: When someone cheats on you, don't get back with them, because if they loved you, they wouldn't have done it in the first place... once a cheat, always a cheat.

And rule number two: You need to nip it in the bud straight away.

I do agree with giving someone a second chance, but that has to be it. If the same thing happens again, you have a serial offender on your hands, and these people never change. You can't keep giving the same person more and more chances. You're just lining yourself up for more hurt in the long run, and it'll take you longer to recover. That's all I'm going to say. Trust me, I've been there.

Lots of people still think of me as a really angry person, and I can't blame them, but the truth is, I've calmed down a lot just in the last year. All the things that were making me so angry seem to have gone away. I know that's easy to say, but it's true.

Looking back, it's simple to see what was going on. The bullying had a massive effect on me. The breakup with The Dip was a big part of it too, and the other dickhead exes along the way didn't help. I was around negative people in the Essex scene, who were constantly bringing me down. And I wasn't doing my music full-time.

But now I'm finally doing what I love – writing, recording and touring. And to top it off, I've built my first house in an area I always dreamed of living in, and I really am loving life.

I do realise how harsh I can come across on the TV, and I reckon that's why so many people are wary of me. I've never been able to cry softly on camera. It was always angry crying – you know the look I mean! – and saying really nasty stuff. I know it makes good telly, but it's why people have got me so wrong. When I get emotional, I just don't know how to express it, so it comes out as anger – in fact, it's actually because I'm sad, hurt and vulnerable, all the same feelings that everyone has.

People can still be very wary of me when they first meet me. Only the other night, I was out, I met some new people and we had a laugh. In the cab on the way home after we'd had a great night, one of the boys was slightly drunk, and he said, 'I got you so wrong, Meg.' I said, 'Thank you.' He said, 'You're proper normal.' I said, 'I know.' Ha ha.

You do need to be a really strong character to go on any kind of reality TV show. I know loads of people are queueing up to go on them, but you need to know what sort of person you are before you get in there, or it will break you. I'm strong, and it nearly broke me.

> Another little life lesson I'd like to share is: Don't think that drinking will help you escape your demons.

They'll chase you. All that alcohol was my get-out from being hurt. It gave me a confidence I was lacking. It still gives me confidence, but it's not the answer.

I shouldn't have needed confidence. My family gave me confidence; having those big dreams gave me confidence. But the bullying and heartbreak knocked it all out of me and I'm still recovering.

I do sometimes think, 'Why do people give me such a hard time?' My mum always says it's jealousy. From when I was really young, I've always been able to do my own thing – I was always up to something, ever since I was performing in assembly, belting out a tune. Maybe my life would have been easier if I'd blended in with the crowd, but that's not me. My dreams are big, and fortunately I never gave up. That was because of my family supporting me and believing in me.

I do think now that, if I'd had it easy, I wouldn't be the person I am today. All these dramas I've gone through have definitely made me stronger and more ambitious to do something more with my life. So I would say to any younger person who's feeling unhappy or isolated or unsure of themselves: KEEP DREAMING.

I never stopped thinking about what I wanted to happen. I would say to that little girl, 'Even though you feel like shit now, even if you're at the lowest point of your life, things ALWAYS get better.' And I say that as a girl who was at school, eating her lunch on the stairs, because her special food was getting caught in her braces and everyone was laughing, so you have to believe what I'm telling you.

I've sometimes felt confused, like I don't really know what I want to do any more, but things just always seem to sort themselves out. Something always comes up.

Every time I've got a bit confused, it's because I've been distracted and lost sight of the big picture, so I say as well, KEEP YOUR EYE ON THOSE DREAMS. Me, I got side-tracked by bad relationships that hurt me, friendships that failed and worries about what people thought. It was only when I got back on track and focused on my music that I started feeling happy again. This was around the time of my tour – after Nashville, after *TOWIE*. I didn't have any friends to fight with and a lot of people I thought I loved were no longer in my phone, but I was on the road, singing my music, and that was what did the trick.

Now I know who my true friends are as well. Friends I thought would be there forever have gone, but new ones have come along. The list has been cut in half, and I can probably count the people I totally trust on the fingers of one hand, but that's okay. They know who they are, and they're everything to me.

As far as love goes, what can I tell you? Looking back, I was always too scared to be on my own. I thought I needed someone for security. Hopefully, that's changing now. I'm definitely a lot more independent these days, and I'm definitely not prepared to put up with the kind of shit I have in the past.

I'm now with someone who makes me his number one. My exes never did that for me, and it made me go a bit mad. But equally, it was my fault for not leaving before I did. Oh well, we live and we learn.

Now I'm only prepared to spend time with someone who makes me feel good about myself, one who makes me feel very special. Only then is it worth sharing my heart, and it's worth waiting for, even if it feels like it's taking a while. I can confidently say to anybody else who might ever feel like giving up, 'Don't go looking for love, trust me, you just never know what's around the corner.'

I'm really happy with my life. That's not something I could have said only a couple of years ago, but now I'm in a better place and it's definitely true. There've been some bumps along the way, but I can't say it's been boring and it's all been part of the rollercoaster ride. And as my granddad always used to say to me... all together now... 'Everything happens for a reason, Megan.'

Acknowledgements

Jade Reuben – Where shall I start... how have you not suffered a nervous breakdown from me? I can't thank you enough for everything you do for me, not just as my agent but as my friend too. I couldn't have asked for a better manager. We've been in this together from the start and let's hope it's never gonna end!

The Bold Management team – Jade Reuben, Kate O'Shea, Martin O'Shea, Jackie Christian, Joe Foster, Lauren Bowden, Jason Finegan & Felan Davidson. My amazing agency, thank you for all your help and support.

Caroline Frost – Thank you for being so patient and helping me put my crazy life into words. I know I'm a stress head but at least you've added some new words to your vocab!

Lauren Gardner – My book agent at Bell Lomax Moreton, thank you for keeping everything and everyone so organised!

My publishers John Blake – Thank you for giving me the opportunity to share my story with the world! Special thanks to Kerri Sharp, Ciara Lloyd, Sarah Fortune, Jonathan at Seagull Design, Francesca Pearce, Lisa Hoare, Kelly Ellis and Ben Dunn.

MTV / VIMN

Steve Regan – Thanks for realising my psycho side would be received so well by the CBB viewers. Craig Orr, Kerry Taylor – Thank you for giving me a platform on MTV.

Whizzkid

Sharyn Mills, Sophie Alcock, Jake Court – Thank you for giving me the chance that a lot of people didn't give me. If it wasn't for you, I wouldn't have got my break on TV.

Channel 5 / Endemol

Ros Phillips, Hannah Wetton – Thank you for taking a chance on 'Psycho Megs' and putting me in that CBB house.

Daniella Berendsen – Thank you for believing in me and giving me that chance to show that there's more than just 'Psycho Megs'. If it wasn't for you I wouldn't be where I am today, you made my Nashville dreams come true.

ITV

Paul Mortimer, Amanda Stavri & Rosemary Newell – I love being part of the ITV family, thank you for commissioning my dream show in Nashville.

***There's Something About Megan* team** – Daniella Berendsen, Laura Freedman, Alice O'Brien, Huw Slipper, Craig Pickles, Ceri Hubbard, Kim Nguyen, Hetal Dhanak, Derek Drennan, Harriet Dormer, Shinade Sutherland, Kim Bretton, Cameron Rea, Craig Harman, Jon Kassell, Phil Huberty, Matt Hamilton, Jeremy Mazza & Rachel Hardy – We absolutely smashed it in Nashville.

***The Real Full Monty* / Spun Gold** – Daniela Neumann, Ceri Jones, Kelly Lloyd, Fiona Thompson, Kevin Mundye, Will Yapp, Ellie Hansford, Milly Magwa & Nick Bullen – Thank you for trusting me to be part of this group to raise vital awareness. And of course, my gorgeous *Real Full Monty* ladies; Coleen Nolan, Sarah-Jane Crawford, Victoria Derbyshire, Sally Dexter, Michelle Heaton, Helen Lederer and Ruth Madoc. We raised so much awareness and made friends for life, so happy I got to share this experience with you girls.

Instrumental

Conrad Withey, Emma Banks & Lisa Wilkinson – Thank you for supporting my love of country music.

United Talent Agency

Neil Warnock, Kym Selby, Nick Meinema – Thank you for putting me on the biggest stages that I could only have ever dreamed of being on.

TM – Johnny Buckland – Thank you for your magic potions, you're the best tour manager ever.

My Band

Gary Wallis, Greg Oliveras, Laura Carrivick, Paddy Milner, Rocco Palladino, Michael Blackwell, Linus Fenton, Bob Knight, Loucas Hajiantoni & Luke Marc Hughes – Thank you to my band members past and present, it wouldn't be the same up there on that stage without you guys.

Samantha McWilliam, Carl Bembridge, Jeyanney Calderbank, Beau Babbington & Jack Kenneally – Thank you for being my dream team – my glam squad's better than yours!

Danny De Santos – Thank you for giving me the confidence to work it and for doing my first ever shoots.

Danny Craven – Thank you for smashing every shoot we do. Bring on the future and don't forget to bring the beauty box, ha ha ha!

Glyn & Robert Davies – Thank you for bringing my make-up dreams to life #Mouthy.

Shane O'Sullivan, Joseph Ramos & James Silk @ Easilocks – Who would have thought the whole of the UK would be wearing our 'award winning' bouncy blows!?

McK Grill – Thank you to the team for bringing amazing gluten-free food to Essex.

Mark Manley at Manley's Solicitors – Don't know what I'd do without you... literally.

My Fans – Thank you to my 'Megamaniacs' for supporting me through everything and always having my back, this book is for you!

Mum, Dad, Nan, Granddad, Harry & Milly. Jordan McCarthy & Keely Kane – You guys are my world, not only my family by blood but best friends by choice. I don't know what I'd do without you guys. I couldn't ask for a more supportive family.

Mike Thalassitis – My gorgeous boyfriend, thank you for coming into my life and bringing out the best in me, I love you so much and I can't wait to make more amazing memories with you in the future.

Mum – I have to give you another mention as you've not only been the best mum in the world to me, you're a best friend, therapist, amazing cook and a shoulder to cry on. Thank you for putting up with me.

Picture Credits

MEGAN MCKENNA

Scan the code below on Spotify and follow me
to get access to exclusive music
updates and listen to my latest releases.